FROM SUMER TO JERUSALEM

John Sassoon

JOHN SASSOON

FROM SUMER TO JERUSALEM

The Forbidden Hypothesis

First published in Great Britain in 1993 by
Intellect Books
Suite 2, 108/110 London Road, Oxford OX3 9AW

Consulting editor: Masoud Yazdani
Copy editor: Cate Foster

Designed by Pardoe Blacker Publishing Limited
Shawlands Court, Newchapel Road, Lingfield, Surrey

British Library Cataloguing in Publication data

Sassoon, John
From Sumer to Jerusalem: The Forbidden Hypothesis
I. Title
935

ISBN 1-871516-42-0

Printed and bound in Great Britain by Bath Press, Bath

CONTENTS

LIST OF ILLUSTRATIONS

FOREWORD

PEOPLE SEEM TO THINK that a writing system was essential for the recording of history and gospels. In many cases this was so. However, when a memory system was intact it preserved history better in that it was handed down unaltered as far as it went. This book concerns the distortion of facts that translations and written records can perpetuate. After several thousand years the truth can be so effectively hidden that people are unwilling to accept it even when the facts are undeniable – because all their beliefs are based on the original error. That is why this book had to be written by an outsider.

ROSEMARY SASSOON

ACKNOWLEDGEMENTS

FOR MY KNOWLEDGE of Sumer I am almost totally indebted to those whose works are listed at the end of the book.

I am particularly indebted to Mr C.B.F. Walker of the Department of Western Asiatic Antiquities at the British Museum for reading an early typescript and, despite reservations, making many expert comments and suggestions especially relating to Sumer.

Peter Ford edited a later typescript, and the present version owes much to his pertinent comments. Mr K.R. Gladdish, of the Department of Politics at the University of Reading, read two early chapters, and his comments have coloured the final version. The late Mrs M.H. Waley kindly read an early typescript and made some most useful comments. I am grateful to my daughter Caroline for her advice on Hebrew, and for energetic help with many practical matters.

I am grateful for the patience and efficiency of the staff of the Sevenoaks Public Library and of their parent establishment, the Kent County Library, who obtained, sometimes from distant places, most of the general and some of the specialist books I needed. Much of my research was undertaken in the library of the University of London Institute of Archaeology to whose staff I cannot sufficiently express my thanks.

None of those who so kindly helped me with the text is committed thereby to agreement with my main thesis.

This book could not have been written without the constant personal encouragement of Elwyn Blacker who gave me much needed guidance, irreplaceable support and, always, hope. But it was Rosemary who made me do it and to whom this book is dedicated.

QUOTATIONS

Quotations from the Bible are from the Authorised (King James) Version of 1611 unless otherwise indicated.

The Abbreviation ANET refers to J.B. Pritchard (Ed) *Ancient Near Eastern Texts Relating to the Old Testament.* (1955) They are reprinted by kind permission of the Princeton University Press

INTRODUCTION

WHAT CRIES OUT from a study of Sumer is that the Hebrew/Jewish people are the cultural and probably the ethnic descendants of the Sumerians, creators of the oldest recorded civilisation.

Biblical scholars will not hear of it. Traditionally the Jewish religion begins with Moses about 1150BC, while the Jewish people are said to have begun with Abraham, perhaps 2000–1800BC. Biblical scholars are seldom interested in what may have happened before Abraham. A century or more of modern archaeology has now revealed the very early existence of a high civilisation in the land known as Sumer at the southern end of the Tigris/Euphrates valley in modern Iraq. The tablets make it clear in considerable detail that Sumerian civilisation flourished from before 3000BC until about the time of Abraham, c.2000–1800BC, while the Bible tells us that Abraham was actually born and brought up in Ur, the Sumerian capital city. This Sumerian ancestry is either ignored or discounted by the scholarly establishment, presumably because it would throw unwelcome light on many revered Jewish practices as well as on the central Jewish belief in a single, universal God. But Judaism is not going to be destroyed if some practices previously considered to be entirely religious can also be explained on rational grounds, while belief in a spiritual God is strengthened by being shown to be far older than anyone had imagined.

The sources from which these propositions are drawn are of two kinds: the Bible in its traditional (not its modern) translations, and the thousands of tablets recovered from the dead cities of the main king

Kramer, the distinguished Sumerologist, has led to the discovery that the history of Sumer is after all recorded in the Bible. That story is now told.

Originally the Bible was oral history, memorised word for word, passed from generation to generation for no one knows how long, but for thousands of years at the least. This kind of oral history has nothing to do with hearsay. Its content has been deeply considered and carefully edited. The persons to whose memory that history was entrusted were selected by those who knew them, and knew also the qualities of intellect and character that would be needed to retain and pass it on precisely. Every child in pre-literate societies had the memory trained, as those who have spent time in modern non-literate societies can witness. Memory was not the problem. The content of a controlled memory system was more difficult to alter than a written document because you had to convince a trained and publicly appointed transmitter, the authoritative source, that he was wrong. The written document does not argue, and variations cannot be contradicted until the damage has been done.

From the moment when the Bible was first written down control by the memory system was lost. The original written text has long been lost as well. In the absence of an authoritative text it is little wonder that 'scholarship' has had a field-day. What is surprising is that some translators really do try to get to an authentic text regardless of understanding, fashion or belief.

The evidence that the Hebrew people are the descendants of the Sumerians cannot just be dismissed. But the significance of that claim can only be appreciated if the Sumerians and what they achieved in Sumer are known. That is why the first three chapters are devoted to brief glimpses of life in Sumer starting with its position in time. Where possible the sketches are supported by extracts from published English translations of the actual tablets.

The two main faces of the Standard of Ur. The standard of Ur is a hollow box, triangular in section, decorated with an inlaid mosaic of shell, red limestone and lapis lazuli, set in bitumen. Its use is unknown. It was found by Sir Leonard Woolley in the Royal Graves of Ur and dates from *c*.2600 BC. It is a contemporary illustration of scenes from daily life in Sumer, which shows among many things that the Sumerians wore the kilt.

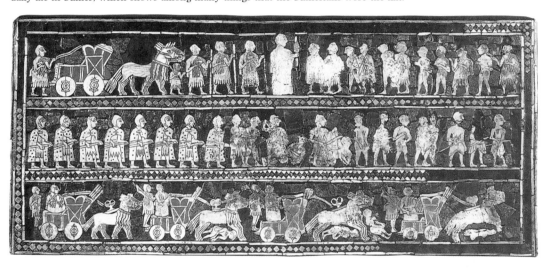

The face of war. This shows, on the bottom line, war chariots charging the enemy. In an incredible representation of movement, the chariots from left to right are shown moving at increasing speeds. The middle line shows prisoners having just been captured. The top line shows the king and his soldiers on the left inspecting prisoners on the right. This reproduction brings out the blue lapis lazuli background.

CHAPTER 1

GLIMPSES OF THE SUMERIANS AND THEIR LAND

The remoteness of Sumer

SUMER WAS A small area at the lower end of the valley of the two rivers Tigris and Euphrates (see map 1). The river courses were slightly different in ancient times, though the shore line of the Gulf has probably not changed much.

Just north of Sumer lay the country of Akkad, which is mentioned in the Bible. The people of Akkad were semitic, and in later times they conquered then absorbed the non-semitic Sumerians.

Such naked facts convey little of the remote antiquity or of the grandeur of the civilisation which the Sumerians created and which, though themselves apparently extinct, they communicated through succeeding empires right down to our own day. To get to the

Map 1: Some of the nations who exercised power during the first three millennia BC.

Sumerians we need almost to close our eyes and sink back through the whole span of recorded history. Even then we can trace only a hazy outline of perhaps the most extraordinary civilisation and people the world has ever known.

It is now nearly a thousand years since William the Conqueror landed near Hastings. Go back as long again and Jesus is walking the Holy Land, preaching in Aramaic to Jews whose own language, Hebrew, had been unheard (except in a religious context) for four hundred years. Here, too, is imperial Rome, conqueror, legislator, disciplinarian, guardian of the peace so long as she remained master of arms. Rome, heir to an older civilisation, studied the Greek language, Greek laws, Greek art, Greek philosophy, translated and adapted the lessons of a still surviving Greece to serve her own contemporary needs. Already the mists hide more than half the story.

Drop back another five hundred years and Rome is unknown, but classical Greece is ablaze with youth, the flame of scientific inquiry already spurting from the embers of ancient mystery. Here great men, Pythagoras among them, have visited Egypt, studied the mathematics and astronomy of Babylon on whose ancient shoulders their own new

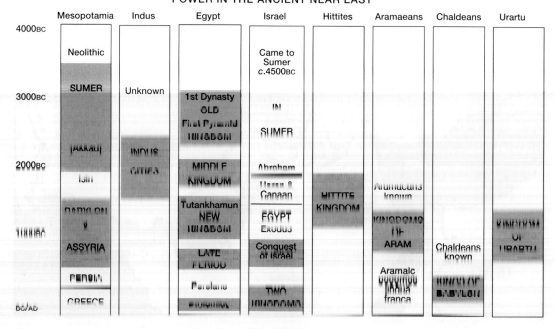

POWER IN THE ANCIENT NEAR EAST

Spouted gold cup, perhaps for feedng an invalid. From the Royal Graves of Ur, *c.*2600BC.

and modern civilisation will be raised; but Homer is already four hundred years ago and Troy as long again before Homer.

While Agamemnon of Mycenae was besieging Troy (*c.*1250BC) the Hittite kingdom ruled in Turkey, Tutankhamun of Egypt was not long entombed in his splendour, and the Jews enslaved under Pharaoh waited impatiently for their Moses, their plagues, their Exodus. Now, too, Aramean immigrants were seeping north from Arabia and settling in Syria where they would found the kingdoms of Aram; while the kingdom of Urartu in eastern Turkey around the mountainous head waters of the Tigris and the Euphrates would soon replace the Hittites and go on to challenge the cruelty as well as the power of Assyria. And down those two rivers, older than any memory, Babylon

But Babylon absorbed her conquerors and made them proud to be her own. It was to Babylon that the ancient near east turned no matter who her kings might happen to be.

Tablets excavated in the cities of Babylonia and Assyria have made it clear that, among the cities of the ancient near east, Babylon was comparatively young. We hear nothing of Babylon before about 2300BC, whereas the tablets tell of cities in the south which were wealthy and belligerent at least seven hundred years earlier; today they are mounds. Archaeology reveals that these mounds hide the ghosts of houses, temples, public buildings, warehouses, schools, and the ashes of the fires that destroyed them; fires that had baked hard the little clay tablets on which they had written their meticulous

THE SUMERIANS AND MESOPOTAMIA

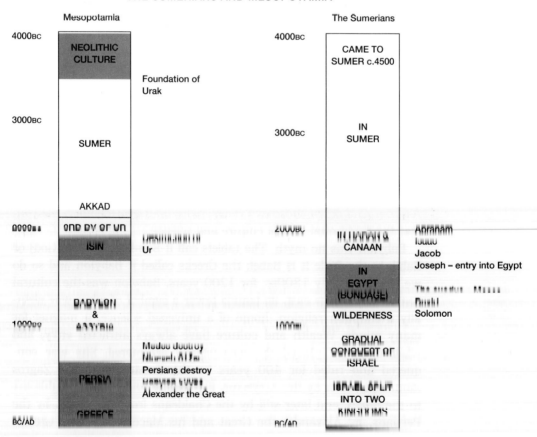

records that permit scholars four thousand years later to peep into their lives. The grey outline of legend takes colour and form, and real people make a noise as they go about their daily business in these cities of Sumer, the earliest known cities in the world.

But in 2000BC the cities of Sumer lay mostly in ruins. Their language survived only as the ancient classical language of learning while their people, absorbed into the semitic background of the Akkadians, were no longer distinguishable as an entity. Four thousand years ago, we are among the ruins of the founding civilisation of the west attested by surviving city walls, statues, inscriptions on clay tablets, and the administrative revelations of tens of thousands of their pedantic financial accounts.

Sumer had flourished as a great civilisation for at least a thousand years before it was destroyed. If we go back to the beginning of their cities, say to 3500BC, we are earlier than Egypt. But to tell the known story of the Sumerians we must go back yet again for another thousand years to about 4500BC when traces of the Sumerians first enter the historical record.

The people of the valley

People had entered the plain of Mesopotamia in the late (neolithic) stone age. They came down the valley from the north or from the Zagros mountains in the east. They left no writing so we cannot say what language they spoke, but archaeology tells us quite a lot about what they did. They were farmers with a settled village economy.

found elsewhere in the region, but it is sufficiently different to suggest the arrival of a people of a higher culture than the neolithic inhabitants.

Time warp back to the end of the last ice-age, say to 10–12000BC. Far to the south, in the middle of the Arabian desert where Riyadh stands today, the air was cool, there was plenty of rain, the land was watered and fertile. People could and did live there. Now let time speed forward. The centre grew hotter, drier, and people began to move out. As the central Arabian desert formed people gradually migrated out of Arabia into Syria and Palestine, but some turned towards the east and entered the valley of the rivers, mingling quite peacefully with the neolithic inhabitants and the Sumerians already there. These are almost certainly the people known to history as the Akkadians. When written history first hears of them they are living in the middle part of the valley just south of modern Baghdad.

Now there are three peoples in that land: the neolithic who came from the north or the east, the Sumerians, and the Akkadians who came from the south and the west.

It is the Sumerians who are mysterious. Were they part of the neolithic people who came down from the Zagros mountains to the north-east or did they come from beyond the Caucasus far to the

Map 2: The Neolithic people arrive in the valley from the Zagros mountains, and Akkadians come in from the desert. The Sumerians appear about 4500BC centred on the city of Eridu.

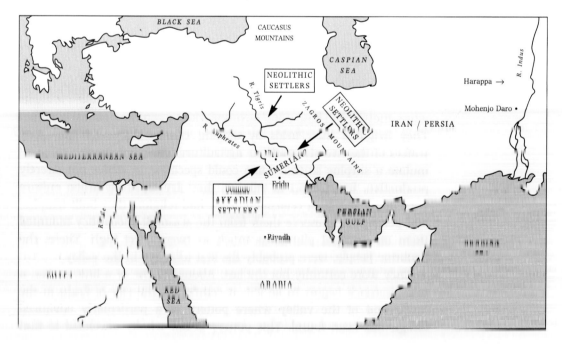

War chariots.
Two-man war chariots, one driver one fighter, are pulled by four onegers. There seems to be a military uniform of kilt, cloak, helmet – possibly made of leather – and bare feet. The infantry are holding their spears in both hands, but in the chariot, bottom left, there is a box of what may be spears which would probably have been thrown. From the Standard of Ur.

north? Or perhaps from the east where lies the Indus valley with its cities centred on Mohenjo Daro and Harappa, dated no earlier than

The land of Sumer

The land of Sumer continues to be flat, low lying and hot. Two big rivers, Tigris to the east and Euphrates to the west, meander sluggishly and muddily for hundreds of miles down the length of that valley, a sort of land extension of the Gulf, 'the land of the two rivers'. The plain is so flat that the rivers spill out into side streams, creating a landscape of water courses, pools, flat islands and tall reeds. From time to time streams, indeed the rivers themselves, have changed their courses stranding high and dry the port cities which had flourished on their banks. Then as now date palms provide both shade and food. Away from the water the land is dusty and hard, but when watered and worked it is as fertile as anywhere on earth.

Both rivers rise in modern Turkey, and not so far apart. With the spring melting of the mountain snows, floods wash down the river valleys, reaching Sumer about June. In ancient times, water spilled everywhere and fields would look like lakes. It was a life-giving flood; but to live in Sumer you had to control and use the water.

The neolithic people controlled the water in a very simple way. They banked up the local streams, then made a small sluice in the river bank which they could open or close; this let the water flow along an irrigation ditch into the fields. Their settlements were usually along the natural line of watercourses, and generally small. Easily manageable local schemes were what they needed. Some of their settlements were larger; indeed, sizable towns grew up and people left the villages to move into them. As the towns grew so the number of villages declined.

The neolithic people built their houses as well as their temples with mud bricks; they had a sufficient agriculture; they had decorative arts; they may even have invented writing; theirs was not a barbarous world. Even so, it is only after the arrival of the Sumerians that we find the first true cities.

The first cities begin to arise a little before 3000BC and are enormous, especially for that age. Many of the early Sumerian cities were founded on the site of neolithic settlements, and some of their names as recorded on the Sumerian tablets, are neither Sumerian nor Akkadian words (for the problem of language, see p. 86). As the Sumerian cities grew so their villages also disappear.

The towns and villages in other parts of the country were undefended, but these Sumerian cities have walls; clearly the people who built them feel a need for a strong place of refuge. Within the walls is relative safety, without, danger; so people flock to live within the walls.

They grow their crops and tend their herds during the day in a wide area around the city, maybe for a distance of eight or nine miles. With perhaps fifty thousand to feed they need that much land, even if it does mean a long journey for some of them. But they mostly come home to the city for the night. They live in the city, and it is there that their crafts, their schools, their literature, their religion, burst into life. Population increased and had to be fed. Small, local irrigation schemes could not support the intensive farming that was needed, so they were replaced by massive enterprises in hydraulic engineering operated by the forced labour of thousands, women as well as men. The Sumerian irrigation systems contrast sharply with those of their neolithic predecessors.

Cities were the cradle of civilisation. Was their original purpose defence, a negative response to pressure from outside? If so, no one could have predicted that confining so many people in a restricted space would act as a nursery for social and individual creativity; but that seems to be what happened. The cities which housed and defended the people and the irrigation systems which fed them were not the creation of spontaneous genius but intelligent reactions to desperate events around them.

Who were the Sumerians defending themselves against? Was it other cities, or a new wave of invaders from the mountains of the east

Mohammed) from which to measure historical time absolutely in either direction. Their king lists, with the number of years in each reign, and their slightly different year lists, provided the only framework within which they could relate historical events to their own day and to each other. We cannot give absolute dates to these blocks of time.

Interpretation of the Sumerian King List is complicated both by some enormously long reigns such as Alulim of Eridu 28,800 years (figures which are not yet understood), and by many of the dynasties which are necessarily listed in succession being in fact contemporaneous. (See Appendix I.)

THE DYNASTY OF KISH

The city of Kish was in Akkad, a little south-west of Babylon, not in Sumer. It was by no means the first city – that honour belongs to Eridu, far to the south – but according to the Sumerian King List it was the first city after the flood to become supreme over all of Sumer and Akkad. It is surprising that, although in Akkad, a majority of the early kings of Kish had Sumerian names.

Later, Kish was sometimes conquered by other cities, and when they did so their kings adopted the title 'King of Kish' indicating that now they were supreme over both Sumer and Akkad. The title 'King of Kish' survived as one of honour and power for centuries after Kish itself had vanished.

THE DYNASTY OF URUK

Uruk succeeded Kish as the leading city. The fifth king of Uruk was named Gilgamesh, and it is assumed that this is the hero of *The Epic of Gilgamesh* who, in the epic, was king of Uruk.

THE FIRST AND SECOND DYNASTIES OF UR

Wars between city states continued incessantly. Perhaps about 2500BC Ur became temporarily more powerful than the rest. This is the period of the royal tombs, excavated by Sir Leonard Woolley whose fantastic treasures are now in the British Museum.

Between the First and Second Dynasties of Ur, the King List men tions kings from Awar, then Kish (again), then Hamazi, then Uruk (again). This does not mean that each was supreme, or that they followed one after the other; they could have, and probably did, overlap.

Similarly, after the Second Dynasty of Ur we find dynasties from the cities of Adab and Mari, before a truly remarkable Dynasty of Kish. This dynasty consisted of one monarch, Ku-Bau, a lady, who started as an innkeeper and ruled Kish 'as king' for 100 years. Four more dynasties are then listed: Kish, Akshak, Kish again, then Uruk again.

THE DYNASTY OF AKKAD

The dynasty of Akkad was the semitic dynasty founded by King Sargon. Sargon appears first in Kish as an infant floating in a reed basket, who was rescued and brought up by a gardener. He next appears as cup-bearer to the king of Kish, when he seized control of the army and conquered the whole of Akkad and Sumer. He built a new capital city, Agade, at or near the site of Babylon. Sargon then ex-

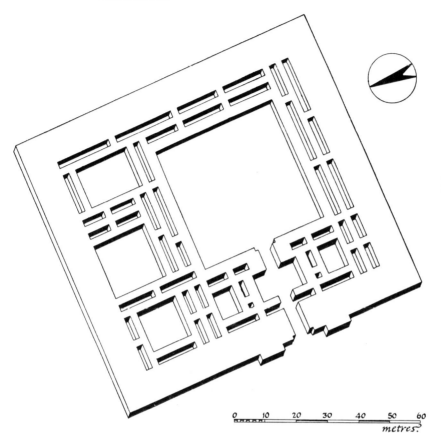

Palace of Naram Sin at Tell Brak. The city of Agade has not been found. This is the plan of the provincial palace of Naram-Sin, fourth kinzg of the Dynasty of Agade just before 2200bc. This palace is at Tell Brak in north Syria.

0   10   20   30   40   50   60
metres.

tended his empire until it stretched from the Persian Gulf to the Mediterranean. The Akkadian period marked a peak in the cultural achievements of the region.

The dynasty disintegrated under attack by the Gutians from the Zagros mountains, possibly the ancestors of the Kurds. After which 'Who was king? Who was not king?' asks the King List, plaintively.

For some forty years before the Third Dynasty of Ur, Akkad and Sumer (or most of them) were ruled by the Gutians.

THE THIRD DYNASTY OF UR

About 2100bc the Sumerians seized back control of Ur and Sumer, then of Akkad. The Third Dynasty of Ur produced the highest of all the achievements of Sumer. But it ended (or nearly ended) after a hundred years with the destruction of Ur by the Elamites from the east, about 2000bc.

THE DYNASTIES OF ISIN/LARSA

When the power of Ur was near collapse, a governor appointed by their last king, Ibbi-Sin, broke away to found his own dynasty in the city of Isin. From Isin, King Ishbi-Erra took control of what was left of Ur. Later, the neighbouring city of Larsa, under a semitic king, Rim Sin, challenged the power of Isin and conquered it. Even so, Sumerian civilisation lingered on during the Isin/Larsa period for 200 years after the destruction of Ur, until the whole region came under the control of Hammurabi of Babylon about 1792BC.

Map 3: Cities and dynasties of Sumer and Akkad.

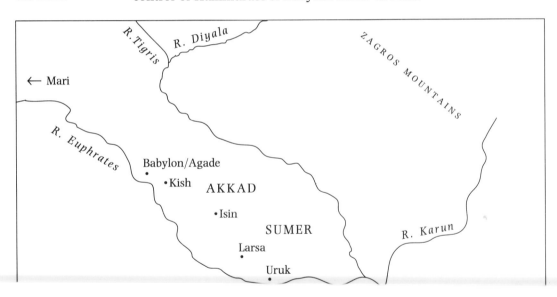

The Sumerians often built their temples on the sites of neolithic temples. Under at least early Sumerian religion, all land belonged to the god, while the king and the civil administration were his agents on earth. So the Sumerian temple was not just the religious but the administrative centre of the region; not just temple, but storehouse and offices; not only priests, but the central civil service. To house all this the temple platform became enormous. The basic design was not so different from the neolithic, but the scale was.

As the temple platform grew to accommodate all the services centred on it, the temple itself was often built on a second, higher platform at one end of the main platform. In time, the number of higher levels increased. The staged temple towers of Sumer, and later of Akkad, were known as ziggurats. When, for a thousand years from about 1800BC, Babil was capital of Sumer and Akkad as well as cultural centre for the whole region, the ziggurat of Babil was the tallest, the grandest and the symbol for all ziggurats. The fame of the Ziggurat of Babil was preserved forever in the book of Genesis, and

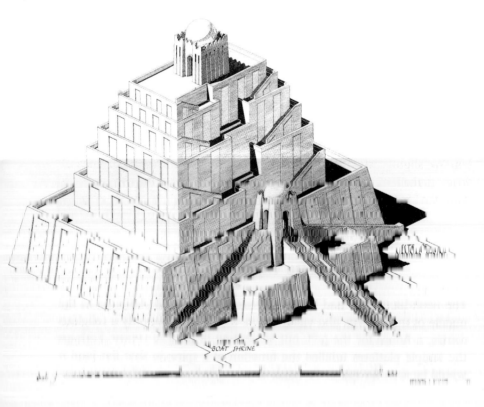

Reconstruction of the ziggurat of Ur according to the restorations by King Nabonidus (reigned c.555–c.539BC, last king of the Chaldean dynasty of Babylon. The biblical Nebuchadnezzar was the second king of that dynasty. Drawn by Majorie V. Duffell in 1937.

**The remains of the
ziggurat of Ur,**
photographed by Sir
Leonard Woolley in
1922. These are,
substantially, the

that story of 'the tower of Babel' was taught to succeeding generations even though, until recently, the modern world knew only part
of what it meant.

From a distance, you would see the huge walls of these ziggurats,

The neolithic brick was rectangular and flat. The Sumerian brick, known as 'plano-convex', was roughly ten inches by six inches, and maybe two inches deep at the edges. It was flat-bottomed, but its top rose in a low convex dome rather like a flat loaf of brown bread; and in the top was a deep hole (sometimes two) made by sticking fingers into the clay when wet. The neolithic brick was laid flat. The Sumerian plano-convex brick was laid on end, slanting, in herring-bone patterns.

Having seen that method of bricklaying used for field walls in Cornwall (England) and spoken with builders, an explanation suggests itself. The slanting lie enables damp to seep down the brickwork, while the space between the bricks demanded by that method of drainage is ensured by the convex top. The alternate slant provided support which was sometimes increased by a line of bricks laid flat

Plano-convex bricks in situ at Uruk c.2700BC.

Cone mosaic at Uruk. A hitherto unpublished photograph by Mr C.B.F. Walker of the British Museum showing cone mosaic (clay 'nail') decoration in situ on a building at Uruk (with dog to indicate scale). Probably just before 3000BC.

beneath a herring-bone row. I have not seen a published explanation of the hole(s) in the top. The herring-bone method of laying bricks was probably developed for drainage, but it was also used decoratively.

Another feature of Sumerian brickwork was the clay cones, sometimes called 'nails'. They were inserted into the face of the brickwork to form mosaic patterns, sometimes coloured. That was certainly a

The cities of Sumer were river ports, so the problem of getting water to their surrounding farms and fields was not quite as intractable as it might have been. The main canals were large enough to take cargo vessels, and the inscriptions record them as being built for transport of grain and other goods between cities rather than for irrigation. No doubt the smaller, but still sizable, canals were used for local transport by smaller boats. To keep the canals navigable they were lined, usually with reed matting held by mud. Silting-up was a problem, so periodically they were cleaned and where necessary re-dug.

At each end of an irrigation canal there was a reservoir, one to control the flow of water going in, the other to allow water to be drained out. So the level of water in the canal was at all times under control. From a main canal there led off smaller canals whose levels and flow were similarly controlled. Such a network around a city had taken years to develop, and it spread over many square miles of country. Its operation and maintenance required an expert knowledge of surveying as well as an enormous labour force. The surveyors were trained in the schools of Sumer. We can discover a great deal about day-to-day work by looking at their records, written in the cuneiform script on literally thousands of clay tablets. They were temple records, dated, signed and sealed, certifying work done as a basis for issuing grain, oil or other goods as payment for the labourers.

> 34 male workers for 1 day compacted the dike of the Ukunuti field
>   and stood with the water to regulate its flow.
> 3 male workers for 1 day compacted the dike of the Abagal field
>   and stood with the water to regulate its flow.
> 8 oar 15 gin of earth filled up at the dike of Oarsubba.
> Foreman: Lugal-murube
> Vla. Ur-Lugal.
> Sealed by. Enkas.
> The year when Shu Sin became king.
>   (Shin Ti Kung, Sumerian Economic Texts from the Umma Archive)

So their labour gangs were organised under foremen who reported to the temple exactly what work had been done. Shu Sin became king of Ur in 2038/BC.

Bitumen

Among the building materials used by the Sumerians was bitumen, which we also know as asphalt or pitch. In the Bible it is called 'slime'. The Sumerians used bitumen much as we do, as a waterproof bonding material. They used it as a mortar for bonding bricks in important parts of their buildings, for sealing their boats and sometimes with reed matting for sealing their canals.

Bitumen lay on or came out of the ground. This is what the excavator of Nineveh wrote over a hundred and fifty years ago:

> On the following day we passed the bitumen pits or the "Kiyara" as they are called by the Arabs. They cover a considerable extent of ground; the bitumen bubbling up in springs from crevices in the earth. It is extensively used for building purposes, for lining the boats on the river, and particularly for smearing camels, when suffering from certain diseases of the skin... (A.H Layard, *Nineveh and its Remains*)

Apart from camels which do not appear until the second millennium, that could be Sumer. In 1964 Wilfred Thesiger reports:

> They also told me that pitch came from Hit on the Euphrates near Baghdad. I had been there and seen small pools where the molten bitumen bubbled out of the ground. After cooling it was sent away in small, hard chunks like the broken-up surface of a macadam road. (Wilfred Thesiger, *The Marsh Arabs*)

226 male workers for 1 day stood with the water and laid bundles
of reeds in the irrigation ditches of the Igi-emabse field.
Foreman: Lu-Shara.
Sealed by Akalla.
The month of the cutting of the barley.
The year when Shu-Sin became king.

(Shin T. Kang, op. cit.)

Although the Sumerians did not invent nylon, their foreman Lu-
Shara could certainly have taken charge of the 1985 'experiment' in
the Norfolk Broads.

Farming

The main food crop was barley. An interesting document known as
'The Farmer's Almanac' has been recovered. It is in the form of advice
to a young farmer on how to grow barley:

...after the sprout has broken through the surface of the ground,
say a prayer to the goddess Ninkilim, and shoo away the flying
birds. When the barley has filled the narrow bottom of the furrow,
water the top seed. When the barley stands up high as the straw of
a mat in the middle of a boat, water it a second time. Water a third
time its royal barley. (Kramer, *The Sumerians*)

The advice is clear, and for once we can see that it was followed, at
least so far as two waterings were concerned:

12 male workers for 13 days irrigated at the field for the first time.
10 male workers for 10 days irrigated at the field, the Manu field,
for the second time.
Foreman: Lu-duga
Sealed by Tirgalimunda
The year when the western wall was built.

(Shin T. Kang, op. cit.)

The irrigation system was not just hydraulic engineering. Around it
if not arising from it, was a whole complex of activity with an appropriate social structure. In some ways this was the heart of Sumer,

CHAPTER 2

GLIMPSES OF THE WAY
THEY LIVED

Inside a city

A WALK AROUND the inner city of Ur during the late third millennium BC would probably not have been very different from a walk around many a medina in a modern middle-eastern town; those terribly narrow streets with no room for wheels and only the occasional donkey squeezing through with its load. Crowds crammed into the lanes between mud-plastered walls often two stories high. The streets provide relief from the glare and blazing heat of the desert but nurse a clammy heat of their own. Shops, shutters open, offer the usual wares: clay pots, leather goods, metalwork, skins, brightly coloured cloths, beads, statuettes of the gods. The shopkeepers, ever keen to bargain, accept payment in measures of barley, or silver – coinage has not yet come. Endlessly and aimlessly twisting lanes are picturesque, but dirty too. Rubbish thrown into the street is trodden in, so over the years the level of the street rises. But the houses are neat inside. You cannot see inside from the street because of a bend in the entrance

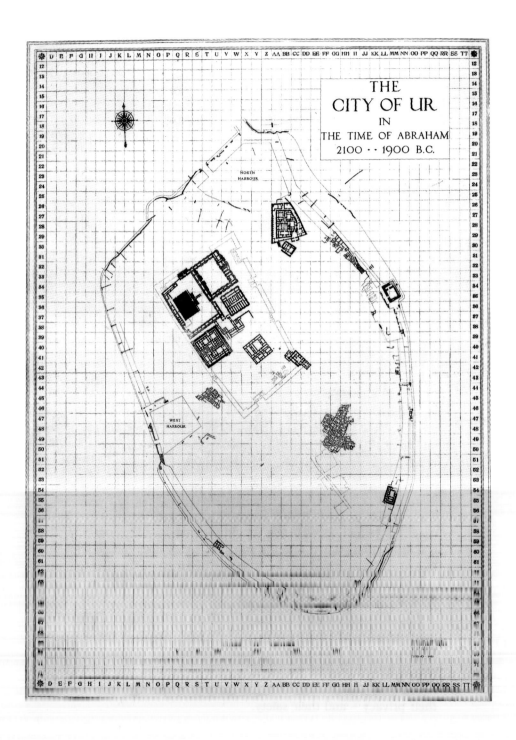

THE
CITY OF UR
IN
THE TIME OF ABRAHAM
2100 · · 1900 B.C.

NORTH HARBOUR

WEST HARBOUR

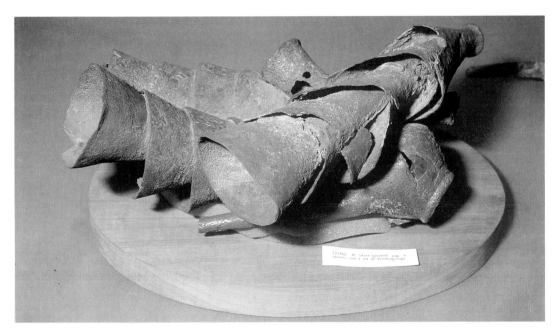

A mass of silver cups with spouted jug, from Ur c.2600 BC. The cups were corroded together and so excavated as one. Possession of a silver service may not have been confined to royalty.

The servants live normal lives with the family. They welcome you with genuine warmth. They fit in. You would scarcely notice that they are slaves.

There are lots of temples in little ends of alleys or just opening off the side of a street. They are quiet inside, but there are always people there. There is an altar and maybe statues, somewhere to sit, to kneel. Not much has changed in four thousand years – only the gods.

Struggling and shoving through the alleys again, we emerge into the glare of the river port: quays, a bobbing of boats, and the crack of rope against masts. Some are large boats, trading down the Gulf into the ocean, west for Egypt, east for the Indus. Smaller boats travel up the rivers and canals with grain or wool for other cities, or they bring down from the northern mountains copper, timber, stone and metals. This is no village. Perhaps fifty thousand people live in Ur alone. Many come from foreign countries: there is colour, movement, a confusion of tongues.

The country is intersected by a network of roads, tracks and pathways. Caravan routes from east and west, north and south, meet and cross in Sumer. The pack animal was the oneger or wild donkey (extinct in the middle east but still going strong in China); the horse had not yet arrived. Along these routes, carried laboriously over enormous distances, came many of the raw materials as well as the consumer goods which made Sumer rich. Even within Sumer a land journey from one city to another would seldom take only a day; so along the road there were inns. King Shulgi of Ur (2094-2047BC) took care of the safety and comfort of travellers:

> I made secure travel,
> built there 'big houses',
> established resting places,
> Settled there friendly folk,
> So that who comes from below,
> who comes from above,
> Might refresh themselves in its cool shade,
> The wayfarer who travels the highway at night,
> Might find refuge there
> like in a well-built city.
>
> (Pritchard, Vol II, The King of the Road)

If you join a caravan made up of onegers with their loads or sometimes carts, you travel for months to cities at the farthest end of the great valley or out, winding through the mountains to modern Iran, Afghanistan or beyond. You may return home with rare woods, metals or stones such as lapis lazuli, the blue the Sumerians loved, but best of all with stories to light the eyes of children who may write them on their school tablets to last for a thousand years, or cause some feminine eye to glow a shade more seriously than hitherto. These great cities, their accurate sharp and stark, pierce the horizon, give shape to the plain. Meandering between them, rivers, streams, canals, all interlaced with pools, islands, reed thickets, and great dark green masses of date palm. There are birds, cattle, sheep; wild animals too, including lion. Date palms dominate the land, endless forests providing shade as well as food.

The trees all belong to someone, king, temple, or even private individuals. But you can walk through. No one is going to worry if you pick a date and eat it, though they might if you put some in your bag. With the sun low in the evening or in the early morning, the plain of Sumer must have glowed in its grandeur. No wonder the Sumerians loved it.

Civil power

The power structure of Sumer starts with the gods; not just as objects of worship but as the source of authority, civil as well as religious. The gods had created the world, and then made mankind to serve their needs; so in theory the city god owned the city and all its land and people. Had that been applied literally, the priesthood would have wielded absolute power; but they did not. Temple and palace were both landowners, as were some private individuals. True, the tablets tell of priests ruling in the palaces of kings, among them the great Gudea, *ensi* of the city of Lagash (*ensi* is a title which is not perfectly understood, but it meant governor rather than king and implied allegiance to another city). They also tell how kings participated in sacred

Civil administration

During the five hundred years from *c.*2500 to *c.*2000BC, the king was always distinct from the temple, and the political authority of the crown became perfectly established. Even so, the temple remained the centre of administration. It was still to the temple storehouses that the annual shipments of grain were sent, and from the temple storehouses that labour was paid. Most of the economic administration remained in temple hands.

The main city temple was not the only temple in a city. In Lagash, about a dozen temple communities organised the cultivation and distribution of most of the barley, the staple food of Sumer. Half the crop went in wages and seed for next year, a quarter went to the king and a quarter was retained by the priests, mostly to be sold. It was the job of senior civil servants to organise this process. Each of the dozen or so temples in Lagash had its own administration, and we know that the name of one of their senior civil servants was Bazi.

Bazi lived in the reign of King Shulgi, second king of the Third Dynasty of Ur, shortly before 2000BC. He had the apparently unexciting job of overseeing the production and distribution of barley, as well as drawing up an annual budget and keeping accounts. Bazi's accounts for the distribution of barley in some years have survived almost intact, and they have been analysed. Grain for wages, grain for animal feed, grain for seed had to be available, and be distributed in the appropriate months; transport, mostly by water, had to be arranged and paid for; and if the incoming harvest differed from the forecast, which apparently it did even in those days, it was Bazi who had to take the decisions for his area. There were at least twelve officials similar to Bazi in the city of Lagash alone, and each must have had a staff with a hierarchy of responsibilities.

Management of the cultivation, storage and distribution of barley meant responsibility for feeding the people of the city; and they had to be fed even if the harvest was poor. But feeding was not the only large public enterprise. maintenance of the irrigation system and repair of the city walls were two more, demanding constant organisation, expenditure and control, on which public safety depended. A city's civil service was complex, and vital to survival. It is no wonder that they placed such weight on the schooling which trained their

administrators in meticulous accuracy and on the hierarchy which ensured discipline. Perhaps this explains how the cities of Sumer maintained their internal structure against every pressure for a thousand years during the third millennium BC.

Trade

The Sumerians could not build with mud brick alone; they needed stone and wood. Their soldiers used spears and wore helmets, and some wore armour; for those they needed metal, usually bronze. For their temples they wanted gold and silver, and ornamental stones such as the glorious, deep blue lapis lazuli. All these had to be imported. Sumer lived by the international trade created by her merchants, financed by temple or palace, defended by her armies, carried in her ships, and conducted according to a growing body of her laws. Sumer's commercial organisation was one of the most astonishing of all her achievements.

Stone and wood came largely from the mountains of Lebanon or Turkey, which they knew as 'the cedar mountains' or 'the silver mountains'. They loaded the stone on to boats, made rafts of the logs, and floated it all down the river. One of the most successful of Sumer's merchant princes was the priest Gudea, Ensi of Lagash just after 2150BC, and before the Third Dynasty of Ur. Gudea was a religious and moral reformer, a restorer and builder of temples, a successful military commander and a director of commercial enterprise. Inscriptions on a clay cylinder tell us:

> In the quarries which nobody had entered before, Gudea, the en-priest of Ningirsu, made a path and thus their stones were delivered in large blocks... (ANET, *Historical Documents*, 3 (Gudea)

Ningirsu was the city god of Lagash

> ...Like ... ships ... were floating down the water of the river from Cedar Mountain, nine rafts from Pine Mountain... (ibid)

The greatest of all the trade routes into Sumer were the Euphrates and Tigris rivers. Imports could be floated down them, but exports had to be carried by land up their valleys. The boats they used were built in the hills, and either dismantled or sold on arrival in Sumer

The world has three main sources of lapis lazuli. Lake Baykal in

An artificial flower from Tell Brak.
Tell Brak is some 500 miles from Ur, in the far north of the Tigris/Euphrates valley, on the Khabur river. The Sumerian outpost in Tell Brak is an example of the early influence of Sumer over distant regions. This elaborate clay 'nail' is pottery with stone petals set in bitumen, and would have been held by its stem in the fabric of the building, projecting outwards. It probably came from a temple façade, as part of a montage of bulls walking through a flowery meadow.

Siberia, north of the Gobi desert; the Andes mountains in Chile; and Shar Shakh in Badakhshan, in the north-east corner of Afghanistan. The Shar Shakh lapis lazuli is the rich, dark blue used in Sumer, and archaeology tells us that lapis lazuli has been mined in Shar Shakh for at least four thousand years; whereas the lapis lazuli from Siberia and, incidentally, Chile, is of a different colour and quality. The Sumerians might have seen the Shar Shakh lapis lazuli in markets nearer home and arranged with traders for a supply; but it is likely they maintained their own mining communities on site, manned mostly by slaves. Records of resident Sumerian trading communities are found elsewhere in the near east.

Copper could have come from many sources, and no doubt did. It is found in the mountains of north-west Iran, in the Caucasus, in the mountains of eastern Turkey; and it is found in Oman. Tablets from Ur around 1800BC tell of a thriving trade in copper with Dilmun, the name given at that time to a walled city outpost of the Indus civilisation on the island of Bahrain.

Three foreign lands are named in the tablets as perhaps the most important of Sumer's trading partners; but Dilmun, Meluhha, and Magan are not easily located. Dilmun may at that time have meant, or included, Bahrain; Meluhha has been a candidate for Ethiopia as

Map 4: Trade and raw materials.
The question marks against Dilmun reflect doubt about where Dilmun was. In later years it probably referred to the island of Bahrein, an outpost of the Indus Valley civilisation, but it may originally have referred to the Indus Valley itself.

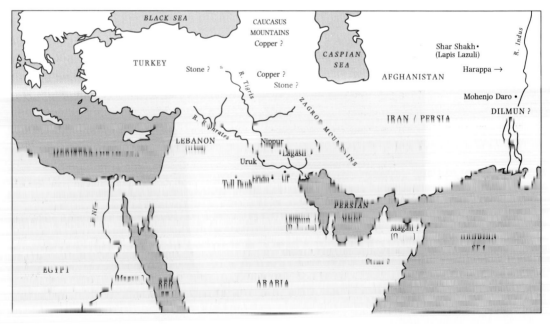

well as the Indus valley, while Magan has been associated with Egypt, as well as with Oman which is almost certainly the source of the black diorite used in later Sumerian sculpture. An inscription about Sargon of Agade describes his overseas trade around 2300BC:

> At the wharf of Agade he made to moor ships from Meluhha, ships from Magan, and ships from Tilmun (ANET, *Historical Documents*, 1. Sargon)

In exchange for her imports, Sumer exported agricultural produce including grains, wool, woollen cloth, hides, and leather goods; but not all of Sumer's transactions required an exchange. Many of her imports were received as tribute imposed by conquest undertaken, at least in part, with that end in view. The Sumerians knew well the economic as well as the military value of superior arms, and made sure their army was equipped with modern weapons. War fought to obtain sources of raw materials has a long history.

A framework of law

Law is the framework of society. Without a legal framework no community can exist. What can we say about the ancient laws of Sumer? Would we be willing to obey them today? Some of them certainly not; but others are timeless such as laws against theft or violence, or laws requiring that the truth be told. Many people have the impression

Ancient laws were less comprehensive than ours; they placed more weight on individual circumstance and leaned heavily on the discretion of the judges.

There are other differences. When we talk of 'the rule of law' we seem to give law a life of its own, to turn the law into a remote, inflexible deity complete with priesthood, ritual and reverence. By contrast, the early law codes look very like summaries of what sensible judges had in fact decided in particular cases, brought together to act as a guide to their courts and an indicator to their public. Ritual was certainly used to overawe in temple and palace, but there is no evidence that it was used that way in Sumerian courts.

In Sumer, judges were not full-time professionals. They had jobs like other people, and were selected as judges part-time by virtue of their known character. Some scribes no doubt will have specialised in giving legal advice much as solicitors do today; but there is no sign of a barrister, a professional advocate.

Each Sumerian city had its code of laws. These codes were inscribed on tablets and placed where they could be seen, although most people would need a scribe to read for them. The early codes which have survived from Sumer are not the originals but later copies, sometimes by schoolchildren as part of an exercise; but there can be no doubt that they are accurate. Only the great code of Hammurabi is engraved on stone, and only that code has survived almost intact. The codes are:

The laws of Ur-Nammu. Ur-Nammu was the first king of the Third Dynasty of Ur. It now looks as though these laws may have been written by his son and successor, Shulgi (2094-2047BC); but they continue to be known by his father's name. The laws themselves date from about 2100BC, but the school copies which have survived were made around 1750BC. They are written in Sumerian.

A law fragment. A school exercise dating from about 1800BC. The laws copied are very fragmentary, but are clearly Sumerian laws. They are written in Sumerian.

The laws of Eshnunna The laws of the city of Eshnunna in Akkad. They date from just after the destruction of Ur, about 1975BC, and they are written in Akkadian.

The laws of Lipit Ishtar. Lipit Ishtar was the fifth king of the

King Hammurabi of Babylon, sixth king of the first dynasty of Babylon, reigned *c.*1792–1750BC. The provenance is unknown, but the inscription suggests that it is contemporary. Hammurabi is shown in relief, dedicating a votive inscription to a goddess. The sculpture dates from about 1750BC.

dynasty, and city, of Isin. He reigned from 1934 to 1924BC. It was in Isin that Sumerian civilisation lingered on after the destruction of Ur about 2000BC. These laws date from about 1930BC, and they

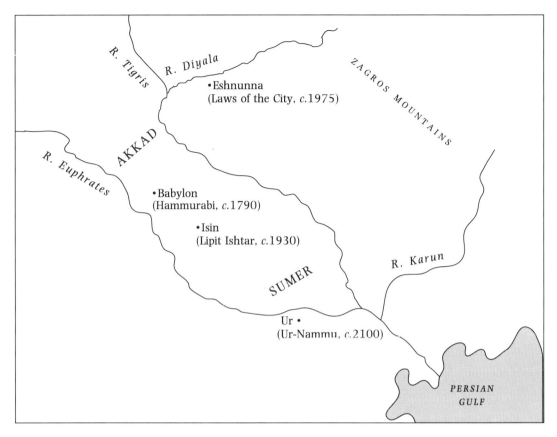

held at the city gates. Three judges were usual, though sometimes there were fewer. There was a court clerk, among whose duties was writing the court record. A number of these records have survived, of which this is one:

Map 5: Early law codes.

> Sur-DUB.UMBISAG swore by the king's life that by the new moon of the month of Eating the Malt he would produce the thief of Lu-Nanna's stolen sheep; and if he did not produce him he would be a thief.
> Before Sur-Ig.alima, son of Kagu; before Kagina, the messenger; and before Shesh-Sheshgu the overseer,
> Month of the sowing, 11th day,
> Year the Simsh had chose the high priest of Inana.
> Seal: Sur-DUB.UMBISAG scribe, son of Utugu, chief of the weavers.

It is curious that the court clerk should have the same name as the accused, but they are unlikely to have been the same person. The judges are identified by their occupations or social status. This record does not seem to disclose any injustice.

The status of women

Some societies idealise 'masculine' characteristics such as command and discipline, adventure and heroism; others, less common among 'developed' countries, lean towards the more 'feminine' characteristics of nurture and culture. A predominantly 'masculine' society will be very protective towards women, but will often emphasise their separate and inferior status by an almost ceremonial courtesy. A more 'feminine' society will idealise activities which tend to the creation of life, to the care of persons, or to the cultivation of resources in which women will participate as a matter of course on an equal footing with men. All societies will wage war, and from aggressive as well as defensive motives; but the more 'feminine' society will be less likely to produce war poetry. All societies contain both 'masculine' and 'feminine' elements but they strike different balances, and a woman may well be accorded privileges and find her life easier in a mainly 'masculine' society.

A distinction must be made between the position of women in a society based on truly 'feminine' principles, and their position in one based on 'masculine' principles in which women may seek, and be allowed to live, what is essentially a man's life.

In any age the gods reflect the ideals of mankind. In the Sumerian pantheon, the thread of femininity starts with the goddess Ninhursag (who was equally called Nintu). Ninhursag was not only the mother of the gods, but the goddess of motherhood. Her place among the

Ninmu was a goddess in the Sumerian paradise land of Dilmun, in which this poem is set. Ninhursag, or Nintu, is referred to as 'the mother of the land', and the poem goes on to tell how she was also impregnated by Enki to give birth to some of the plants:

> She took the semen into the womb, the semen of Enki.
> The 'tree'-plant sprouted,
> The 'honey'-plant sprouted...

(ibid)

and so did six other plants. This poem, incidentally, tells us that it was forbidden to eat the plants in Dilmun; and that when the god Enki did eat them, he was cursed for doing so by Ninhursag, who would have nothing more to do with him. Ninhursag did not create the world or mankind, but she gave birth to some of the gods and, as mother of the land, gave birth also to some of the plants; and she represented motherhood in the Sumerian pantheon.

Dumuzi, the fisherman (according to the King List), or shepherd (according to the myths), who was fourth king of Uruk and Gilgamesh's predecessor, was said to have married Inanna, queen of heaven and goddess of love. This myth gave rise to the principal ceremony of the Sumerian year: the New Year ceremony, celebrating the holy marriage of the king with a temple priestess representing Inanna. That was considered necessary to ensure the continued fertility of both people and crops in Sumer. As the Sumerians were practical, as well as imaginative, a consummation actually took place.

Only slightly lower than the gods, two powerful ladies appear in the tablets. The Sumerian King List tells of a remarkable dynasty in the city of Kish. Not only did it consist of a single monarch, but that monarch was a lady called Ku-Bau, who started as an innkeeper and ruled Kish 'as king' for 100 years, until the city was defeated in battle.

Enheduanna, daughter of Sargon, king and founder of the Akkadian dynasty, was appointed by her father as high priestess of Nanna the city god of Ur. Enheduanna wrote (among other works) a hymn to Inanna, goddess of love, queen of heaven and city god of Uruk.

Not many years separated these two ladies; they may even have lived at the same time, in which case they would have known each other. But Ku-Bau, the Sumerian, sounds like a woman leading a man's life, and very successfully; while Enheduanna exercised power as well as influence from a mature position in a women's world — and

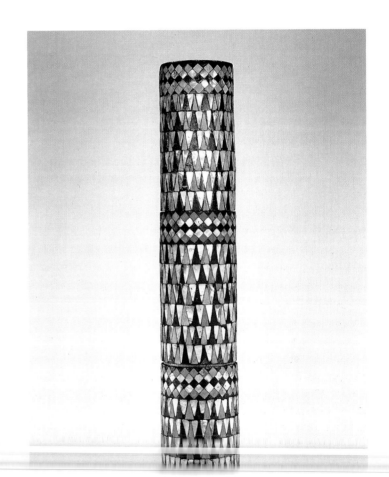

it is Enheduanna, the poetess, who is best remembered.

At the other end of the social scale, a Sumerian court record tells us about a woman slave – or servant. Nurtured on the history of slavery as practised in Europe and America, we find it surprising that a slave in ancient Sumer could challenge his status in a court of law. That a woman slave should be allowed to do this is astounding; and yet, a perfectly equal treatment of women with men when a crucial point of definition was at stake, fits well enough into the pattern of attitudes if 'feminine' principles are respected, as they undoubtedly were in the Sumer of before 2000BC. This court file from the reign of King Shu-sin, c.2030BC, complete with the names of the judges, reports a case brought by the woman slave Ninkuzu. Her action was unsuccessful; but Ninkuzu in presenting her case and the judges in hearing it, were scrupulous to observe the laws of Sumer, particularly those relating to the need for witnesses.

Ninkuzu, daughter of Sur-Nanse, a servant of Atu the diviner, appeared before the court and declared:

'By the King's name, this is the position: Within two days I shall produce witnesses that Nasaba, a son of Atu, has freed me. If I do not produce them, let me be a maidservant to the heirs of Atu!'

Because on the appointed day as per her oath by the King's name Ninkuzu did not produce witnesses to her having been freed, the maidservant was assigned to the heirs of Atu.
Lu-uruka was the bailiff.
Lu-digira, Sur-Istarana and Lu-digira were the judges.
Year king Shu-Sin erected the lofty stela of Enlil.

(Edmond Sollberger, *Some Legal Documents of the Third Dynasty of Ur*)

A fascinating sidelight on the persistence of the 'feminine' principle in Sumerian memory is found in their erotic (or at any rate, love) poetry, of which they had quite a supply. We have long been used to poetry, novels, plays films television which portray the physical beauties of young ladies mythical and real, all written from the point of view of the man. What we are not used to, and what we find in Sumer, is erotic poetry written from the point of view of the woman. It may of course have been written by women contemporaries, high priestess of

Ur and daughter of King Sargon of Akkad, whose surviving hymn to Inanna is not erotic, would hardly have been the only woman poet. The erotic poetry was love poems, or passages in myths, largely concerned with gods, heroes and, of course, heroines. An unkown bride of King Shu-sin of Ur before 2000BC, starts her poem:

> Bridegroom, dear to my heart,
> Goodly is your pleasure, honey-sweet...
> ...You, because you love me,
> Lion, give me, pray, of your caresses...

(Kramer, History Begins at Sumer)

The Enki and Ninhursag myth about the creation of some of the gods and plants is written, in very plain language, from the point of view of Ninhursag. As woman rather than man was the creator of life, so perhaps the 'feminine' principle rather than the 'masculine' was seen as fundamental to human society.

The high status and wide opportunities open to women in Sumer greet us as a surprise when we first encounter them, and we attribute to the Sumerians a more modern attitude towards women than may, perhaps, be justified. The liberality with which women were treated and the aspirations they were allowed to entertain, derived from the survival in their religion and their society of the 'feminine' characteristics associated with the worship of the goddess of motherhood and fertility. But these were being inexorably replaced by a 'masculine'

A Glance at the family

A glimpse of the young is all that the tablets give us, and even that is indirect such as these excerpts from a poem about a schoolboy which is clearly written by an adult:

> When I awoke early in the morning,
> I faced my mother and
> said to her: 'Give me my lunch, I want to go to school.'
> My mother gave me two 'rolls', I left her;
> my mother gave me two 'rolls', I went to school...
>
> I spoke to my father of my hand copies, then
> read the tablet to him, and my father was pleased;
> truly I found favour with my father...

(Kramer, Schooldays)

Father is head of a nuclear family in which mother keeps house and sees to the children. The schoolboy son presses his mother for his lunch in case he should be late for school – the poem later tells he was in fact late, and was caned for it. In the evening it is to his father that the boy shows the tablets he has written in school that day, and it is his father's approval that matters to him. Younger children had toys. The clay animal on wheels is a design still to be bought in almost any high street toyshop; and although the gaming board came from the tomb of a king, many homes will have had a plainer board on which parents and children played together. Life inside the home has hardly changed.

To catch a glimpse of how Sumerian society regarded their children, we have to rely on Hammurabi and the ancient laws he included in his code. The principles underlying these laws are very old indeed. Children were the most personal of all property. They were truly owned, which is how most of them like it to be, and the law took pains to keep them safe and let them grow. The whole future of Sumer was rooted in the family, and the quality of family life determined the character of the child. Children must be cherished but not coddled, and they must learn the self-control essential to living in a relatively small community. The Sumerians loved their children but refrained from worshipping them.

Two Sumerian laws on a school exercise tablet around 1800BC, probably recording a long established tradition, state the duty a son

A Sumerian toy animal on wheels, from a low stratum of the Royal Cemetery of Ur c.2600BC. This design is still available on every high street.

owed to his parents as well as the duty his parents owed to him; they recognise that love alone will not preserve the family and make it work. The first law makes it clear that when the Sumerians spoke of discipline, they meant it.

> Law 4. If a son said to his father and to his mother: 'You are not my father; you are not my mother,' he forfeits his heirs rights to house, field, orchard, slaves, and any other property, and they may sell him into slavery for money at full value.
>
> (Pritchard, Vol. II, Sumerian Laws)

It was not all one-sided:

> Law 5. If his father and mother say: 'You are not our son', they will forfeit their estate.
>
> (ibid)

Those two laws recognise the intense emotions that can inflame a family, and they provide strong sanction against letting those emotions get out of hand.

Disinheritance was a public matter. To some extent it still is. Hammurabi's two later laws (below) on disinheriting children, strike an almost exemplary balance between the exasperation of a father, his duty to tolerate the impudence of youth, and a youth's duty to learn that being intolerable means, simply, that he will no longer be tolerated; and they rely on judicial discretion informed by the second millennium BC equivalent of social reports.

> 168. If a seignor, having made up his mind to disinherit his son, has said to the judges, 'I wish to disinherit my son', the judges shall investigate, and if the son did not incur wrong grave enough to be disinherited, the father may not disinherit his son.
> 169. If he has incurred wrong against his father grave enough to be disinherited, they shall let him off the first time; if he has incurred grave wrong a second time, the father may disinherit his son
>
> (Pritchard, Vol I, The Code of Hammurabi)

There is nothing tyrannical about that.

Writing

Perhaps the most significant of all Sumerian skills was that of writing. No one knows who invented writing. Tablets similar to those of early Sumer have been found widely in Mesopotamia and Iran, but Sumer was the first civilisation that could be called truly literate even though the majority probably could not read or write. The school was called *edubba*, meaning tablet house; the students were *dumu-edubba*, sons of the *edubba*, and the learning taught in the *edubba* was known collectively as the scribal art, *dubsarra*. *Dubsarra* included the whole range of professional knowledge essential to a scribe, practical as well as theoretical, but the first and central subject in the *edubba* was writing.

Human memory and oral instruction had brought the Sumerians a long way, but these were not enough for the changing records and communications which a city economy, a civil service and a growing science would need.

How did writing come to be? There is no agreement about what writing is, though we can be reasonably sure about the main steps that led from the drawn sign to the written sentence.

From about the fourth millennium BC stamp seals and cylinder seals, carved with signs, had been widely used to indicate ownership. Impressed or rolled on clay, they left an imprint of what was really a personal trade mark. They were used to identify goods sent by way of trade. Often little inscribed pebbles of clay were enclosed in a clay

Early pictographic tablet, provenance unknown. A record concerning barley; the holes are numerals, c.3200-3000BC.

and associated ideas, and they are then usually called hieroglyphs. Thus a star in pictographic writing might mean a star but as a hieroglyph it might represent heaven. We are now well before 3000BC.

A hieroglyphic script conveys ideas direct without needing words, even across language barriers. Road signs today exploit these advantages. But it is not easy to work out the language spoken by those who used either a pictographic or a hieroglyphic script. If we draw a picture of a leaf, everyone would understand it; but to an English speaker it would be 'leaf', to a French speaker '*feuille*', to a German '*Blatt*'. The picture does not tell you the language of the artist. That is why we do not know what language the earliest Mesopotamian picto-graphic script was written in. Many think it was Sumerian, but no one can be sure.

If you are confined to hieroglyphs, a very large number of different signs will be needed. A different sign for each idea means that thousands of signs have to be memorised. So the Sumerians began to give phonetic value to their hieroglyphs. People do not make so many different sounds, though they string the sounds together in many different ways.

The alphabet is a phonetic script, so are the various systems of shorthand.

Once signs are given phonetic values it is possible to write down what people actually say. A phonetic script can record a language complete with its grammar. The first phonetic scripts were based not

ɔn single sounds but on syllables. The first phonetic script was cuneiform, the writing of the Sumerians. It started before 3000BC and by about 2500BC it had been refined into the form which was to last until the time of Christ. The cuneiform script had about 600 signs in normal use.

The alphabet with fewer than thirty letters, each (supposedly) representing a single sound was probably invented about 1700BC in north Syria. Thereafter the alphabet and cuneiform existed side by side, the alphabet slowly gaining ground and cuneiform slowly losing it. The last cuneiform document to have been found was written about AD75.

A glance at the school

Of all the tablets dug up by archaeologists from the city mounds of Mesopotamia none are more astonishing or revealing than those from the ancient schools. Here are the children's textbooks, their dictionaries, their mathematical problems; here too are their own exercises, including copies made by them of their traditional legends, poetry and laws – often the only copies to have survived. We can even read a few of their original letters home to their parents.

Schools were for boys, and both schools and boys could be tough. Standards were high, discipline strict. In the third millennium BC children generally hated school.

Only a few fortunate, or privileged, children could go to school. Schools were sometimes attached to a temple, but it seems they were more often held in private houses. In either case the curriculum was secular rather than religious, though religion played a considerable part in it. Schoolchildren today would probably recognise their predecessors of four thousand years ago. This extract from a boy's letter to his mother has a familiar ring to it:

> ...I am sitting behind the door of
> the Great Music Hall eating garbage,
> may I not die from it

(Ali Fadhil Abdulwahid, Sumerian Letters)

If the edubba was to produce the professional men needed, its curriculum had to be appropriate to the needs of the economy and society of

Sumer. Writing always came first; the speed, accuracy and clarity with which they could produce a written tablet was a matter of competition:

> You dolt, numskull, school pest, you illiterate, you Sumerian ignoramus, your hand is terrible; it cannot even hold the stylus properly; it is unfit for writing and cannot take dictation. And yet you say you are a scribe like me.
>
> (Kramer, *The Sumerians*)

That comes from a tablet recording an argument between two students, a literary genre popular in the ancient world.

Writing, mathematics, literature, music were the core subjects. In addition there were vocational subjects, including surveying (land and quantity), law, and accountancy. Teaching methods were formal, and often based on word-lists. These were tablets listing the technical terms used in each subject, and the suggestion is that the students had to copy those lists in perfect detail and learn them by heart. Many word-lists have been recovered from cities all over the ancient near-east, including lists of plants, of medical remedies (though without symptoms their meaning remains obscure), of animals, of legal terms;

but among the most useful for the modern world have been the bi-lin-gual word lists translating the Sumerian language into Akkadian.

In early times the language of instruction was Sumerian. In later years, particularly during the dynasty of Sargon of Akkad (*c*.2300–*c*.2100BC), the Akkadian language began to predominate until it became the daily spoken language of Sumer. But Sumerian remained the language of learning, if not of instruction, and one of the most important tasks facing a student during the last part of the third millennium BC was to learn Sumerian. They had a proverb:

A Scribe who does not know Sumerian, what kind of a scribe is he?
(Gordon, *Sumerian Proverbs*)

The Sumerians counted in 10's as we do but only up to 60. Above 60 they started again with one bundle of 60, plus so many 10's and units until they reached 60 again when they had two bundles of 60, and so on. That kind of scxagesimal system has some advantages: for instance, one-third of 60 is 20 but one-third of 100 is an endless deci-mal.

The Sumerians probably invented place notation, under which the value of a figure is determined by its place in a series of figures. For instance, by themselves 3 means three and 2 means two, but put them together and 32 means three tens and two units; reverse them and you get twenty-three. The Sumerians did not stop at whole num-bers; they continued the series into fractions as we do decimals, and that allowed them to handle complex questions easily. For '0' they left a blank which was mathematically accurate, clear enough in the mid-dle of a number but ambiguous at the end, though they did know the difference between 6, 60 and 600.

The invention of place notation also meant that all numbers could be represented by just ten numerals, 1 to 9 and their version of 0.

Their mathematical problem tablets throw an interesting light on their teaching methods. The facts are set out briefly: a square kiln burnt brick, the length of its sides and its height given; how many bricks needed for a given job? Or a little canal; length, width and depth given, the volume dug by one man, and a man's wages in bar-ley; how many workers are needed to dig it and how much are their wages in barley? What we find curious is that the correct answers are given at the end of each problem. Perhaps Sumerian teachers consid-ered that the right answer was of little importance compared with the

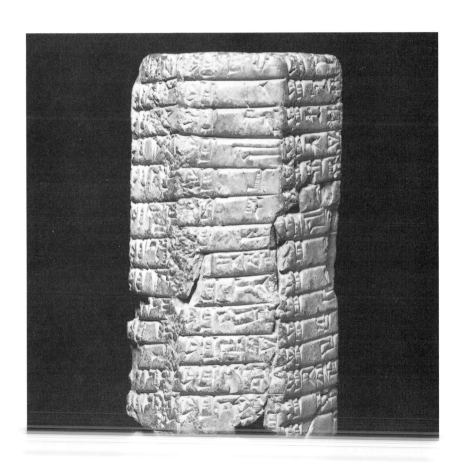

right method of calculating, and that giving the answers allowed the students to check their work for themselves and made guessing impossible. If that is what happened in Sumerian schools their methods were considerably in advance of most of our schools, and virtually all our examinations, today. This tablet tells about practical work in surveying:

> Go to divide a field but you won't be able to hold the tape and the measuring rod, the pegs of the field you won't drive in, you are not able to figure out the sense.
>
> (Sjöberg, *The Old Babylonian Edubba*)

Education in Sumer was not all vocational. Not only surveying but music, literature, religion were also important. 'Do you know the samnu instrument, the timbuttu, the harharu and the inu-instrument' asks one tablet; King Shulgi, second king of the third dynasty of Ur entered the temple '...and took charge there of the tigi music, the sweet', says another.

The *edubbas* must have been mainly middle-class schools. They charged fees, and prepared boys for 'white collar' careers. Perhaps a few poorer boys might have gone there on charity, but not many; and not many sons from ruling families either, because the scribal careers for which the *edubba* would prepare them were not really those of ownership and command. Even so, the scribe was often destined for high office in the civil service or for responsibility on the land, be it royal, temple or private estate; and he was expected to acquire the personal qualities such as loyalty that go with an office of trust. A scribe who betrayed his trust could expect no sympathy, as this surprisingly modern proverb confirms:

A chattering scribe – his guilt is great. (Gordon, *Sumerian Proverbs*)

The scribal art, *dubsarra*, was no narrow expertise in handwriting; the scribe *dubsar*, no mere secretary, but a man of learning and culture. The copying of detail enabled the Sumerians to preserve their past, gave order to their observations and initiated the young into habits of truth; while a strict regime gave their lives both form and goals. Skills were learnt, creative arts were practised and studied; and, if mischief had to be curbed, it obviously existed. Children may have complained, but growing up in Sumer must have been fun.

Religion

The Sumerians were religious in a sense in which we can understand it. They had developed the concept of a personal god which clearly reflected profound and ancient religious experience. It was not dependent on the observance of any exclusive ritual, and was compatible with worship of a public pantheon to which it was indeed related.

The Sumerian pantheon represented their understanding of the controlling powers of the universe, among which fertility was pervasive. After the gods had come into existence they created the world, then they created mankind to serve their needs. But they miscalculated, because man turned out to be disobedient, selfish and, if the Babylonian myth, Atrahasis, is reliable, noisy:

> ...Oppressive has become the clamour of mankind.
> By their uproar they prevent sleep
>
> (*Atrahasis*, trans E.A. Speiser, ANET 1955 p. 104)

Exasperated, the gods decided to destroy man by a flood, but that was another miscalculation because one of the gods gave the game away and a Sumerian Noah built an ark.... There is something only too human about the Sumerian gods.

In early times the most powerful god was An, god of heaven, but he was later superseded by Enlil, god of air and affairs on earth. Ninhursag, also called Nintu, was mother goddess and goddess of motherhood. Among the other gods was the goddess Inanna, city god of Uruk, queen of heaven, god of love and storms. In Akkadian times Inanna was merged with the semitic goddess Ishtar and associated with war, not least by Enheduanna, daughter of Sargon of Agade, poet and high priestess of Nanna who was the city god of Ur.

> In the van of battle, everything was struck down before you,
> My queen, you are all devouring in your power.
> You kept on attacking like an attacking storm ...
>
> (Pritchard, Vol. II 1975, Hymnal Prayer of Enheduanna p. 127)

The Sumerian Inanna had never been one to shrink from a fight, but whether she had been god of war in pre-Akkadian times, or even whether the Sumerians had a god of war, is not fully certain.

Some of the gods were also patron gods of cities, Inanna of Uruk we have just met. Enlil was god of Nippur, the holy city but never the capital of Sumer; Enki, god of water and wisdom, was god of Eridu, while Nanna, god of the moon and also son of Enlil, was the city god of Ur.

In addition to the named gods, great or minor, there were two faintly sinister communities of gods whose individuals were unnamed. The Annunaki, children of An, god of heaven, operated from the underworld controlling fates and acting as judges. The Igigi were shadowy but terrifyingly powerful in an undefined way.

The Sumerian pantheon influenced, if it did not father, the later religions of Babylon, Assyria and Palestine, so that with local variations, particularly in names, what was virtually a common religion spread over the whole of the ancient near east. Religion, unlike greed or ambition, was not yet a reason for war.

The religion of Sumer contained two surprising features, of which one has proved to be of fundamental importance to religious thinking ever since. The first, the *me's*, were certainly unique. They were a collection of abstract qualities related to, or underlying, all aspects of life. They were sacred, and were under the charge of Enki, god of wisdom:

> Enki... speaks up with authority:
> My ancestor, the king of all the lands,
> Gathered together all the *me's*, placed the *me's* in my hand.
>
> (Kramer, *The Sumerians*)

... and made a gift of the *me's* to his daugh-

torical importance is their worship of a personal god in addition to the regular gods of the pantheon. The world is used to early religions, which (more or less) correctly identified the natural forces controlling human life and personified them as gods whose conduct was partly human. The resulting pantheon and its myths attempted to supply man's need for certainty in a world where truth is not to be found. But the established religions of the modern world, every one of them more recent than Sumer, are far from used to acknowledging that peoples hitherto dismissed as heathen, pagan, or idolatrous, had found their way to a personal and spiritual god centuries before even the oldest of their prophets. Abraham is dated sometime between 2000 and 1800BC; at least five hundred years before Abraham, around 2500BC, the Instructions of Shurrupak make it clear (in a partly reconstructed passage) that worship of a personal god was even then a part of Sumerian religion:

> To your father's words like to the words of your god, may you pay attention.
>
> (Alster, *The Instructions of Shurrupak*, Abu Salabikh Version)

The gods of the pantheon related to the power centres of society. Kings, generals, high priests, individuals when acting in public life, had dealings with the great gods who, in turn, dealt principally with them. By contrast, the personal god was a spiritual presence inside each person, private, intimate, approached and feared secretly, sensitively from within.

A person's god was often nameless, though not always. Those born to power or influence might have one of the great gods also as a personal god. There are no statues of a personal god, he had no features, he was spiritual; but a man knew his personal god, and knew that his personal god knew him.

The personal god was inherited at birth from the father, and was in a sense the spiritual father of the child. When a man said he worshipped the god of his fathers it was not just a statement of religious practice, not just saying that he believed in the god his father believed in; it was an affirmation of his personal origin and identity, as organic and inescapable as birth itself of which it was part. Whatever your religious beliefs in general terms might be, you could no more escape from your personal god from the god of your fathers, than you could escape from any other fact of life.

A man's personal god might intercede on his behalf with the great gods, but he was no easy friend; you ignored or disobeyed your personal god at your peril: 'The destruction is from his own personal god; he knows no saviour', says a Sumerian proverb (Gordon, *Sumerian Proverbs*). A much later poem about a man and his personal god has survived, Man and his God (Pritchard, Vol. II, trans S.N. Kramer):

> Let man utter constantly the exaltedness of his god,
> Let the young man praise artlessly the words of his god...

If the young man had done wrong his god would leave him, and life would then be bitter and desolate:

> My god, you who are my father who begot me, lift up my face...
> How long will you neglect me, leave me unprotected?

Let the young man confess and his god would forgive:

> The man – his bitter weeping was heard by his god...
> prayerfully confessed ...
> ...and his god withdrew his hand from the evil word.

The personal god inherited from the father was the individual's private guide, judge and defender in a world of vast and unknown forces. The personal god was one of the company of gods, and possessed knowledge of their ways not given to any human being. As

That they may believe that the Lord God of their fathers, the God of Abraham, the God of Isaac, and the God of Jacob, hath appeared unto thee. (Exod. 4:5)

To the Hebrews at the time of the Exodus the true God was identified as the God of their fathers. A thousand years earlier the Sumerians had uniquely identified their personal god as the god of their fathers. If that is a coincidence, it is a rare one.

CHAPTER 3

THE END OF SUMER

The destruction of Ur

SOMETIME around *c.*2150BC the Gutians (possibly the ancestors of the Kurds) came down from the Zagros mountains, conquered Akkad, destroyed the city of Agade and ended the Akkadian dynasty. They then ruled Sumer and Akkad for forty years. About 2100BC the Sumerians at last reasserted themselves, drove the Gutians back into their mountains, reclaimed their cities, made Ur for the third time capital of Sumer, and established their rule not only over Akkad but over lands far to the north as well. The Third Dynasty of Ur lasted only a century, from *c.*2100 to *c.*2000BC, but it was the climax of a thousand years. The city states were at the peak of their prosperity; the temples and their ziggurats, the arts, all that made the quality of their lives, flourished as never before.

Map 6: The final assault on Sumer.

GUTIANS

During the reign of Shu-Sin, fourth of the five kings of the Third Dynasty of Ur, semitic Amorites from the western deserts, whom the Sumerians regarded with derision, swept in and were first recorded as a danger to Sumer. The Sumerians called them 'the Martu':

> The Martu, the people of the lord that knows not grain ...
>
> (Pritchard, Vol. II, The Curse of Agade)

Shu-Sin, like the later Chinese and the Roman Hadrian, built a wall one hundred and sixty-five miles long, to keep them out, but they came in nonetheless.

The Amorites were not by temperament invaders and destroyers. Like the Akkadians before them, they were emerging from Arabia looking for land where they could settle and live. The great plain of the two rivers lay open, beckoning, where plenty of their fellow Amorites had long lived in peace with their neighbours. But this time, their numbers and their way of life threatened the established city societies, and they found themselves harried. They could not return to the desert, so the clash had to come; and when they were attacked, they fought.

While the Amorites were fighting the Sumerians for their lives and their future, and the Sumerians were fighting the Amorites to preserve an established way of life, an altogether different kind of invasion was launched against Sumer from their rear. In a broad valley that eats into the wall of the Zagros mountains, lay the country of Elam. Sousa, the capital city of Elam, was almost as old as Ur and, although not Sumerian, had developed alongside Sumer a civilisation that was almost indistinguishable. Like so many close but different neighbours, the Sumerians and the Elamites were traditional enemies, raiding each other's countries and destroying each other's cities whenever they thought they could extract plunder with impunity. Sumer's problem with the Amorites was predictably insoluble. In Sousa and as the Sumerians fought danger to the west, the Elamites pounced from the east.

It was a coincidence rather than a combination of enemies that destroyed Sumer in 2000 BC. Watching the progressive havoc wrought by the Amorites and Elamites the Guntians, the defeat of their forty-year reign still smarting in their minds, descended once more from their mountains to join in the plunder. City after city fell to invaders; and while the end was still precariously held off, the time

tiers of the Sumerian empire were rendered meaningless and the city of Ur stood virtually alone. Even so, King Shu-Sin, who died in 2029BC, and his benign but ineffectual successor, Ibbi-Sin, held final disaster at bay for a few more decades.

During this period of progressive disintegration, it was Ibbi-Sin's governors, looking to the safety of their cities and their own ambitions, who began to wonder where their future lay. Ishbi-Erra was one of those governors. He wrote to Ibbi-Sin, warning that the Elamites were the danger before whom he must not weaken, but threatening that he would only send grain to his king if he were given command of the cities of Isin and Nippur. King Ibbi-Sin does not seem to have been impressed, because shortly after this, when Ur was destroyed, King Ibbi-Sin vanished as a prisoner in Elam while Ishbi-Erra re-appeared as king of the city of Isin.

In the event, Ishbi-Erra was right. It was the Elamites who destroyed the city of Ur.

The destruction of Ur around 2000BC is notable partly for the momentous consequences which followed from it, and partly for the fact that the destruction of Ur had a chronicler. A poet-scribe, writing some time later, has left tablets containing one of the most poignant descriptive works of any age, a vivid portrayal of the scene inside the city of Ur while the destruction was actually taking place. The text of this poem (ANET, *Lamentation over the Destruction of Ur*, trans. S.N.

temples that the gods should spare their cities, spare Ur from destruction. As their cities were not spared, the gods must have intended to destroy them. For the destruction of Ur, the Sumerians blamed the gods:

> The utter destruction of my city they directed ...

The assault gathers force, like a storm.

> Over the black-headed people, the winds swept; the people groan.

The city walls are breached:

> Its walls were breached; the people groan.
> In its lofty gates, where they were wont to promenade, dead bodies were lying about;
> In its boulevards, where the feasts were celebrated, scattered they lay.
>
> In all its streets, where they were wont to promenade, dead bodies were lying about;
> In its places, where the festivities of the land took place, the people lay in heaps...
> Its dead bodies, like fat placed in the sun, of themselves melted away...!

There was no one now to care for the wounded:

> Its men who were struck down by the spear were not bandaged...

Terror kept the people in their houses, where they starved or were burnt to death:

> Ur – its weak and its strong perished through hunger;
> Mothers and fathers who did not leave their houses, were overcome by fire
> The young lying on their mothers' laps, like fish were carried off by the waters

The citizens understood that it was not only people who were dying, their whole society was dying too:

> The judgement of the land perished; the people groan.
> The counsel of the land was dissipated; the people groan.

The scene of abandonment was heartrending:

In the city the wife was abandoned, the child was abandoned, the possessions were scattered about.

The public stores were plundered:

In all its storehouses which abounded in the land, fires were kindled...

Ekishnugal, the temple of Nanna the city god, was torn down:

The lofty unapproachable mountain, the Ekishnugal -
Its righteous house by large axes is devoured...

...the righteous house they break up with the pickaxe; the people groan.
The city they make into ruins; the people groan...

The enemy tear down the brick built houses:

My houses of the outer city they have destroyed – 'alas for my city' I will say;
My houses of the inner city have been destroyed – 'alas for my house' I will say...

The rivers and canals which brought life to Sumer are breached, their channels are dried, the workers have vanished, and wild animals begin to make their homes in the canal banks:

Temples and houses hacked to pieces; what used to be streets, choked with corpses; families split apart; young men, girls, children captured into slavery; the very bricks pickaxed into the earth; devastation, and then desolation. What had been the city of Ur, reduced to a mound of blood and rubble.

Departure from Sumer

Picture a few tattered, shocked survivors staggering out of the smoke. Who else was alive? They knew that their king, poor Ibbi-Sin, was a prisoner on his way to Elam, and that most of the leading citizens had been identified and slain. Only small groups of dazed people drifted together some way from the still smouldering ruins, wondering what they could do now. The simple things were going to be hardest: what would they eat? How would they live? Each was stunned by the loss of wife or husband, child or parent, friends.... No hope ever of seeing again those not with them now; gone were those who had been so much of all they had loved and worked for, even sometimes feared... gone.

The cities had fallen. Even that would not, in former times, have meant the end of Sumer. What turned disaster into catastrophe now, what this time made it impossible for even resilient Sumer to rise again, was the simple but devastating fact that the Sumerians had virtually ceased to exist. It was not their belligerent enemies but their companion Akkadians who dealt the soft but fatal blow. The Akkadians had made themselves masters of Sumerian civilisation and then gently extinguished the Sumerians by peacefully absorbing them.

What could the few Sumerian survivors do now? Over the next days they could look for people and assess the destruction. But what then? With slow, nauseating realism they had to bring themselves to accept that this was indeed the final, bitter end of Sumer. Sumerian civilisation would live on, prospering in the hands of others; but this was the end of the real Sumer, the Sumer their grandparents used to talk about, the creators of civilisation, the discoverers of knowledge. It was the end of the Sumerians. Those who remained would be absorbed into the enveloping body of the Akkadians, and the Sumerians would soon have finally vanished. Even now only a few were left; broken survivors of broken families.

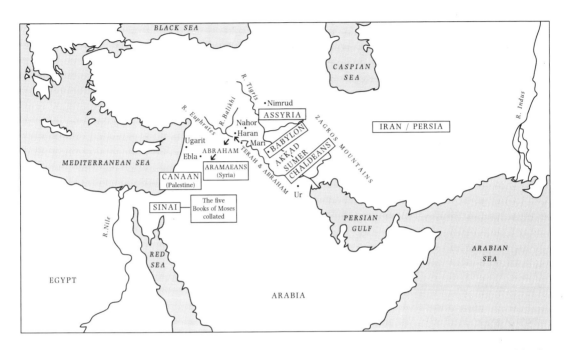

BLACK SEA

CASPIAN
SEA

R. Tigris

•Nimrud

ASSYRIA

R. Euphrates

R. Balikh

Nahor
•Haran
Mari

IRAN / PERSIA

Ugarit
Ebla •

ABRAHAM

•BABYLON
AKKAD
SUMER
CHALDEANS

ZAGROS MOUNTAINS

R. Indus

MEDITERRANEAN SEA

ARAMAEANS
(Syria)

TERAH & ABRAHAM

CANAAN
(Palestine)

Ur

SINAI

The five
Books of Moses
collated

PERSIAN
GULF

ARABIAN
SEA

R. Nile

RED
SEA

EGYPT

ARABIA

Map 7: The flight
from Sumer as
recorded in the Bible.

Why had it happened? Why had the gods allowed their 'black-
headed' people to die out? Why had the gods abandoned their cities in
the hour of crisis when king, priests and people had cried to the gods
to save them? Whatever reason might be attributed to the gods, the

What would they need to do? First, they would need to keep inviolate their Sumerian ancestry. Second, each must keep alive his awareness of his personal god. Third, they would need somewhere else to live. They could not stay in Sumer and survive as Sumerians because here they would all finally be absorbed by the Akkadians. They knew that in the ancient past, their remote ancestors had found in Sumer a land where they could settle and build afresh. So their first plan must be to do again what their ancestors once had done.

Where would they go? To the south lay the sea; to the east, the heartland of Elam, home of their ancient enemies who had destroyed Ur; to the west, the endless desert where only the Martu lived who were now flooding in to settle in Sumer and Akkad. South, east and west alike were barred to them; only the north offered hope. The ancient trading highway threaded north out of Sumer along the valley of the Euphrates, seeking the mountains of Amanus where the cedars grew, where copper and silver had been mined before being floated on rafts down the great river to Sumer. That route had water all the way, and all the time; the terrain was not too difficult for women with their children, and the men and boys could look after the few animals they might take with them. There were cities in the north. They knew Mari, where Ishbi-Erra had been born; they knew Haran, too, the provincial capital and trading centre so far to the north that it might provide a haven, at least for a time. North was the way to go; Haran their immediate aim.

It would be a desperate enterprise; but for the moment, it was enough to remember that they had come through fire, and emerged welded into a group. They were all Sumerians; each had his personal god, and so knew the assurance of inner support. They had that determination, known to the desperate, which would impel them to walk together, north out of Sumer, out of Akkad, far from all their homes to find a new land where they might cherish and revive the spirit of Sumer. Determination would set them on the road, but only discipline would keep them united year after year, century after century. The means to enforce discipline had still to be established, but the skeleton of a strategy was already in place, to guard their Sumerian ancestry, and worship their inner, personal god.

Telling the rest of the story

At some time within two hundred years after the destruction of Ur *c.*2000BC, say 2000–1800BC, the Bible makes it clear that a small party set out from Ur for the city of Haran on their way to Canaan, and that they were known by the names of their leaders, Terah and his son Abraham. Terah and Abraham may not have been the only group to have left Sumer around that time, but they are the only group of which we have a written record.

Haran (or Harran, or Charan in the Latin alphabet) was a well known provincial capital in the north, on the banks of the Balikh river, a tributary of the Euphrates. The route from Ur followed the ancient trading highway, five hundred miles up the west bank of the Euphrates to its junction with the Balikh, then another hundred miles up that tributary. The journey, with animals and children, would have taken between two and three months. Haran still exists. It is on the Turkish side of the Syrian/Turkish border and is marked on the atlas. The party stayed in Haran until Terah died, then moved south into Canaan (Palestine/Israel).

In Canaan they were pastoralists, herding and grazing animals. With no settled home they accumulated wealth but not power, so they do not appear in contemporary non-biblical records. During the period of six hundred years between Abraham and Moses, the Bible

to keep them ethnically and socially distinct as a people, and they clothed those practices in religious authority to ensure they would be continued after Sumer had been forgotten. That strategy succeeded. The Sumerians had always had an intense religious streak reflected in their unique religion. This spiritual awareness was not created at, nor interrupted by, their departure from Ur. Even at that date their religion was already astonishingly close to what it was eventually to become.

When putting this possible scenario to today's world there are problems. Religious authorities can forgive those who deny their mysteries, but not those who explain them. Academe does not like being invited to re-think a long and lovingly tended subject on completely new principles and from the very beginning. We live in an age so terrified by the consequences of doctrines of superiority that we suspect separation in any form or at any level. So the barriers go up.

That the Hebrews have preserved their cultural identity, and possibly much of their ethnic identity too, for four thousand years is accepted. To attempt to explain this in twentieth century terms is hard enough; to expect people to listen to that attempt is optimism run riot. Even so, there is a story here. The longest survival story in recorded history must be worth telling in the light of today's evidence, and if ancient record and modern archaeology suggest that four thousand years is too short, that too needs to be said. In fact, the evidence suggests that the Hebrews have survived as an identifiable people for at least six and a half thousand years and that their past contains periods of greatness no one had suspected.

There are many ways in which this story might be told, but if reason be accepted as more cogent than romance, let it emerge at least in outline from a brief study of its sources.

CHAPTER 4

THE HEBREWS AND THE SUMERIANS

ONE TEST of a possible relationship between the Hebrews and the Sumerians is whether the biblical sources for the Hebrews and the extra-biblical sources for the Sumerians agree with each other more closely than can be accounted for by coincidence. Sources of each kind can be compared for three periods whose dates are nothing like as certain as they look:

PRE-SUMER until *c*.3500BC. From the age when the Sumerians might first be identified until the beginning of the first Sumerian cities.

SUMER *c*.3500–*c*.2000BC. An outline history of Sumer in the Bible.

POST-SUMER *c*.2000/*c*.1800BC–*c*.1150BC. From Abraham until after the Exodus.

There is a preliminary general point. Like the Sumerians, nobody really knows who the Hebrews were, but a detached look at the sources, biblical and extra-biblical, can give us some idea of who they were not. They were not, for instance, Aramaeans. Abraham, ances-

Septuagint were popularised texts in circulation in Palestine at that time and perhaps seeming suitable for the purpose for which the Septuagint was intended. The Hebrew texts, from which the traditional Hebrew Bible derives, are generally later than the Septuagint, but they maintain an older tradition and are considered more authoritative.

A study of the editing processes can shed light on some passages, but the date at which a particular passage was incorporated into the biblical text does not fix the date of the passage's content, nor bear upon its authenticity. The historical matter that was allowed into the early biblical texts was as accurate a reproduction as possible of traditions which had been preserved meticulously in oral form, some of them for thousands of years. An oral tradition which includes an editing process and training in the recitation of detail is generally more accurate and far more difficult to tamper with than a written document.

The King James (Authorised 1611) version of the Bible says that originally the Hebrew people came into Sumer from the east:

> And it came to pass, as they journeyed from the east, that they found a plain in the land of Shinar; and they dwelt there. Gen 11:2

That is the crucial text. For at least two thousand years before the end of the last century, no one knew for certain where Shinar was,

Map 8: The Aramaean migrations.

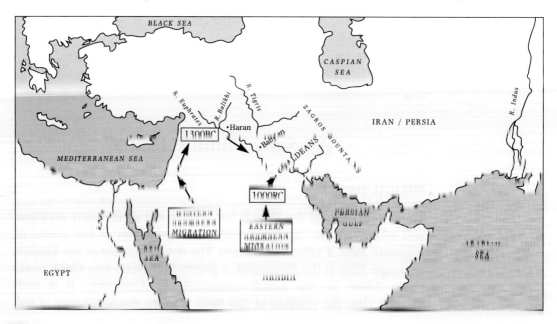

though it was assumed to be in the region of Babylon (see Appendix, Midrash Rabbah, c.AD400–500). But nobody tampered with the text of the Bible or altered it to conform with scholastic fashion. As a result the ancient tradition was preserved. When archaeology confirmed that Shinar was Sumer and Akkad together, the biblical text was intact and its meaning could at last be understood. That meaning is that the Hebrew people came into Sumer and Akkad from the east. Arrival from the east has an important implication. The semitic peoples came from Arabia which is to the west or south-west of Sumer. People who came into Sumer from the east could not have been semitic.

In a pedantic sense the Hebrews can be said to be semitic, because 'semitic' literally means speaking a semitic language, that is, one of what we know as the Arabic family of languages. Hebrew is a semitic language, so the Jewish/Hebrew people are described as semitic. But if it can be shown that, in addition to having come into Sumer from the east, their original language was non-semitic, then the ethnic and cultural connotations of being 'semitic' do not apply to the Hebrews and use of the term 'semitic' to describe them becomes misleading. In fact, Sumerian was a non-semitic language. It gradually ceased to be the spoken language of Sumer over a period of some five hundred years ending about 1800BC, which was also a late date for Abraham. Abraham and his group left Ur between c.2000 and c.1800BC. They must already have spoken (semitic) Akkadian before they left because

The Jewish translation of 1917 according to the Massoretic text reverses the ancient tradition completely with its rendering 'as they journeyed east'. If you journey east, you are coming from the west. Thereafter, translators divide. Following the 1917 precedent, one Jewish text (the 1950 translation of the Pentateuch and the Haftorahs) said 'from the west', while three Jewish texts stayed with 'from the east' (the 1959 Pentateuch, the 1964 Anchor Bible translated by the eminent Akkadian scholar E.A. Speiser, and in 1981, The Living Torah, translated by Rabbi Kaplan of New York). The six non-Jewish texts split, or perhaps splinter, two to 'from the west' (the French and the English Jerusalem Bible), two were non-committal (New English Bible and the Cambridge Bible Commentary), and two stayed with 'from the east' (Moffat and the Revised Standard Version). The question is about history not doctrine, and there is nothing sectarian about the division. In this one phrase the public is now confronted by a scene of disarray.

Biblical scholarship is concerned partly with the history of the text of the Bible and partly with the text itself. The study of the text is again divided between its wording and its meaning. In ancient times the wording had priority; the text was not altered merely because it was not understood. In modern times, from and including the Revised Version of 1881–86, supposed meanings have increasingly been given priority and the text of the Bible has been altered on that basis. In this particular case, 'from the east' is used consistently from c.250BC to AD1611, and it has continued to be used intermittently ever since. Change starts in 1881–86 when we find 'in the east', then in 1917 'east', while in 1968 'now as they moved eastwards', completes the reversal. In the few cases where reasons are given for a change, they are in terms of modern scholarship not of textual integrity.

We can only speculate about the reasons for changing the translation into 'eastwards' or, effectively 'from the west' Perhaps it involves a circular argument: because Hebrew is a semitic language, the Hebrews must be a semitic people; the semitic people came into Sumer from the west, not from the east; therefore 'from the east' is an error which 'scholarship' has a duty to correct. That argument overlooks that the non-semitic Sumerian language ceased to be spoken at about the period Abraham left Ur, so when he left he was almost certainly speaking a semitic language (Akkadian). In face of this, language cannot identify the Hebrews as a semitic people. In the future

and cultural senses of that word. The phrase 'from the east' is in fact perfectly consistent, and there are no grounds for changing it. This whole incident demonstrates that if 'scholarship' is ever allowed to prevail over accuracy the truth about our oldest heritage will be lost.

It is reassuring that the most modern Jewish text, The Living Torah of 1981, states clearly 'When (the people) migrated from the east, they found a valley in the land of Shinar, and they settled there.' Let us hope that that will set the record straight - in two senses.

At the end of the day there is one fact: that the most ancient tradition we have for the origin of the Hebrew people says that they came into Sumer from the east. And there is one final thought: ancient traditions which have been preserved unaltered for thousands of years have an uncomfortable habit of turning out to be based on a core of truth.

Extra-biblical sources

A biblical tradition that the Hebrews came into Sumer from the east does not identify them as Sumerians, but it is significant. The next question is whether there is extra-biblical evidence that the Sumerians came into Sumer from the outside, and if so from where. For this we

Map 9: Shem and Sumer.

ACHAEANS   BLACK SEA

must look at the tablets and other archaeological remains from Sumer, Babylon and Assyria, which relate to the origin of the Sumerians, and also at the views of experts about them.

Scholarly opinion is divided. Some (e.g. Finegan 1979, p.17; Kramer 1963, p.42) hold that the evidence for a cultural break indicates that the Sumerians may have come into Sumer from elsewhere, while others (e.g. Joan Oates 1979, p.21; Roux 1980, pp.88–9) consider that the evidence for continuous development within Sumer from the earliest times is strong enough to suggest that the Sumerians were a group of the original neolithic people.

Five fields are of particular importance to this discussion: pottery, bricks, the continuous occupation of sites, the origin of cities, and language.

POTTERY

About 4500BC a new and advanced design of pottery appears on the site of the future city of Eridu (Melaart 1975, p.170). On the other hand, advanced pottery of similar age has been found in neolithic centres to the north and could have arrived in Sumer by way of trade, sparking a local and similar industry (Roux 1980, p.70). The argument from pottery is undecided, but inclines towards 'development in Sumer'.

BRICKS

The differences between the Sumerian plano-convex brick and the other bricks in use at that time have already been described (Chapter 1). They were different building technologies. Of course, in theory a group of the neolithic people might have invented the plano-convex brick while their use of it went undiscovered or did not survive, but the evidence at present suggests that the neolithic people did not invent or use the plano-convex brick.

Nor did the Akkadians, normally. But the plano-convex brick has recently been discovered in the Akkadian city of Eshnunna (modern Tel Asmar) dating from either before the Agade dynasty (c.2300BC) or from its very early days (Harriet Crawford 1991, p.87). This may well reflect the intermingling of the Sumerian and Akkadian peoples and cultural exchange between them.

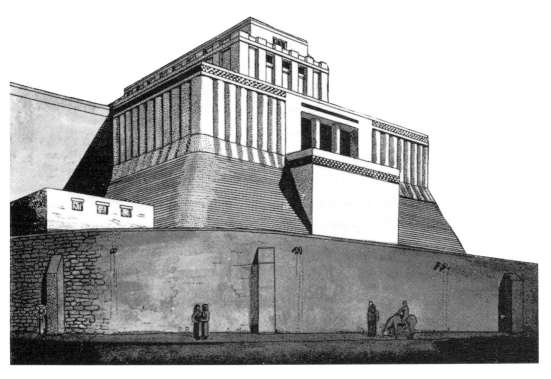

The temple at Eridu. A reconstruction of the

The plano-convex technology was used mainly during the early years of the Sumerian period (before *c.*2500BC), and only occasionally

among. The evidence from continuous occupation is consistent equally with the Sumerians having been a group of the original inhabitants, or new arrivals who settled in before producing their cultural leap.

THE ORIGIN OF CITIES

In early times, say before 3500BC, the area of Sumer and Akkad was peppered with small agricultural villages interspersed with a few larger settlements or towns such as Ur, Uruk or Eridu. During the period *c.*3500 to *c.*3000BC, the larger towns in Sumer grew into recognisable cities equipped with defensive walls. These cities attracted the rural population from their surrounding countryside to come and live within the walls, while continuing to cultivate their fields during the day. In Sumer, the movement from country into city was virtually complete by *c.*3000BC. In Akkad, their neighbours to the north, none of this happened. The Akkadians continued in their villages and towns, and built no cities, until very much later (Adams 1969, p.117). The neolithic people never built cities. This pattern suggests cultural differences between those who built the Sumerian cities, who we call the Sumerians whatever their origin, and the Akkadians and the neolithic people.

THE DYNASTY OF KISH

Sumerian and Akkadian were both written languages which have survived (more or less). The neolithic language(s) were not written and have not survived. Akkadian is an inflected language related to Arabic, hence semitic. Sumerian is an agglutinative language in which words are built up mainly from monosyllables, not unlike Turkish and some African languages; but it has a unique vocabulary unrelated to any other known language. Sumerian is not related to Akkadian it was not a semitic language (nor was it Indo-European), and its speakers could not be described as semitic.

The possible relationship between Sumerian and neolithic languages is more difficult. S.N. Kramer, the eminent Sumerologist, tells us (Kramer 1963, p.41) that the names of early Sumerian cities such as Eridu, Ur, Kish are not Sumerian words – nor are they Akkadian. The words used by the Sumerians for such common occupations as farmer (famer) herdsman (nanar), metalworker (whitesmith) and many others are not of Sumerian or Akkadian origin. The Sumerian words for the rivers Tigris (Idiglat, but, aware of a consonantal alphabet, note the biblical Hiddekel in Gen 2:4) and Euphrates (Buranum) are neither Sumerian nor Akkadian words. This language pattern is consistent with the Sumerians having arrived as immigrants in Sumer, adopted the local names for settlements, common occupations, certain geographical features, and objects, for which they would need names understood by the original inhabitants, but it is inconsistent with the hypothesis that the Sumerians were themselves the original local population.

SUMMARY

The discussions of pottery and of the continuous occupation of sites are indecisive, but building technology, the evolution of cities, and language at least make a case for suggesting that the Sumerians may have come into Sumer from outside. The archaeological evidence would not make this impossible. If they came from outside Sumer, where might they have come from? Did the Sumerians have any legends which might give a pointer?

Dilmun was the paradise land of the Sumerian gods, and it was also a country with which Sumer traded by sea. Nobody knows for sure where it was.

A clue to the direction of Dilmun lies in the flood stories. The oldest

story of the flood. After the flood, Utnapishtim, the Babylonian Noah, was granted eternal life in the ancient paradise land (the name Dilmun is not used), and Enlil said,

> ' ...Henceforth Utnapishtim and his wife shall be like unto us gods. Utnapishtim shall reside far away, at the mouth of the rivers!'
>
> (Pritchard, Vol. I, The Epic of Gilgamesh, trans E.A.Speiser)

In spite of recent identification of Dilmun with the island of Bahrain which was an Indus trading post (Bibby 1970, *passim*), Kramer (1963, p.281) considers it more likely that Dilmun was the Indus valley itself, where from *c.*2500BC the cities of Harappa and Mohenjo Daro and their surrounding towns flourished. But those cities were too late for the origin of Dilmun so that cannot be the whole story.

Assuming that these two flood stories have a common basis, the Sumerian 'the land where the sun rises' places Dilmun in the east and implies far away. From Sumer, Bahrain is roughly south-east and only half way down the Gulf which is rather close for 'far away'. The Babylonian 'far away, at the mouth of the rivers' describes the Indus delta, but does not describe Bahrain.

Dilmun was also a real country, whose ships moored at the quays of Agade during King Sargon's Akkadian dynasty. If a people promote a real country into a paradise land of their gods, it may indicate a tradition that their remote ancestors came from there. 'The Sumerians refer to a sacred land called Dilmun, "where the sun rises", and suggest that they themselves came from somewhere in the east' (Finegan 1979, p.17). The evidence from tradition should not be overlooked. Tradition says that Dilmun lay east of Sumer. It also suggests that the Sumerians as well as the Hebrews may have believed that their ancestors came into Sumer from the east.

CHAPTER 5

AN OUTLINE HISTORY OF SUMER IN THE BIBLE

c.3500–c.2000BC

SO FAR WE HAVE SHOWN that the earliest surviving biblical record of the origin of the Hebrew people says that they came into Sumer from the east; and there is extra-biblical evidence to suggest that the Sumerians may also have believed that their ancestors came into Sumer from the east. That evidence could not prove that the Hebrew people are descended from the Sumerians, but it does make it worth while searching other sources for indications of a possible link between them.

Abraham's birth in Ur (of the Chaldees), the capital city of Sumer, (Gen 11:27, 28, 31) leaves it open whether or not he was a Sumerian. Alternatively, the semitic Akkadians had been in Sumer almost as long as the Sumerians, and by Abraham's birth, c.2000–c.1800BC, semitic Amorites were established there as well and were about to provide

arrived in north Sumer via Palestine and north Syria only about 1300BC, and in south Sumer direct from Arabia still later about 1000BC. That verse may have been composed (or amended) after the time of the Exodus though it refers to a period after the flood. So why does the Bible leave out Sumer?

S.N. Kramer (*The Sumerians*, p.298) provides the answer, now widely accepted. In the cuneiform tablets the word 'Sumer' is in fact 'Shumer', and a linguistic relationship between 'Shumer' and Shem is possible. Kramer then uses the last paragraph of *The Sumerians* to speculate '...If Shem is identified with Shumer-Sumer...' some at least of those who wrote or memorised the material from which the Bible was later collated must have thought that the Sumerians were the ancestors of the Hebrew people. That possibility is not followed up.

In the verse above, the Bible presents Shem as a father, surrounded by his sons just as Sumer was the centre of the family of cultures to which it had given birth. If Shem and Sumer are the same, that picture is accurate and Sumer is indeed mentioned frequently in the Bible.

Genesis, Chapter 11, is the story of Shem and it contains the story of Babel. The Babel story is interpreted in a number of ways including: God punishing man for his pride on earth, and God punishing man for returning to the paganism of his ancestors. The association of Shem with Sumer now reveals that the Babel story (Gen 11:1-9) is an uncannily accurate outline history of Sumer, a factual basis which does not contradict (and could be held to strengthen) the traditional interpretations of it. The historical story of Babel must now be unfolded, even though the first two verses fall well before the strict period of this chapter

Verse 1
And the whole earth was of one language, and of one speech.

Before they entered Sumer, the sons of **Shem** (the **Sumerians**) spoke a common language, implying that they came from a much larger language, and therefore probably ethnic, group. It harks back to a period after the flood when their whole nation was still together, implying that before the flood they had similarly been a single nation

Verse 2
And it came to pass, as they journeyed from the east, that they found a plain in the land of Shinar; and they dwelt there.

This is the story of their coming into Sumer in the first place, perhaps about 4500BC. Shinar is Sumer and Akkad together, and the verse says that they arrived from the east.

Verse 3
And they said to one another, Go to, let us make brick, and burn them thoroughly...

Having arrived in Sumer, they collect material for building. Fired mud brick was a basic building material in Sumer, tougher and more durable than sun-dried mud brick, but more difficult to make. They used fired bricks for the more important parts of their buildings. Verse 3 goes on:

And they had brick for stone, and slime they had for morter.

The scribes, recording this legend in south Palestine in the time of Moses, were used to building in stone rather than brick. Stone was plentiful in south Palestine as it had been earlier in Egypt, while the alluvial mud used for making brick was more scarce. As the scribes were writing around 1100BC, some eight hundred years after their ancestors had left Sumer and at least three thousand years after the ancestors of those ancestors had entered Sumer, they needed to explain that instead of the now familiar stone their remote ancestors

They wanted to make a name for themselves or, in modern terms, establish their identity. To do this, they would create a civilisation which would fix their name forever in the memory of man. The verse then explains why they were so afraid of losing their identity:

...lest we be scattered abroad upon the face of the whole earth.

Having travelled so long and so far, and with the flood an ancient but still terrible memory, the possibility of being scattered yet again and losing their cohesion as a people must have been a national nightmare. In the end, that was just what did happen. Being scattered is a recurrent theme in Jewish history.

Verse 5
And the Lord came down to see the city and the tower, which the children of men builded.

The Lord appears in person, intervenes directly in the affairs of men and reasserts his personal relationship with the Hebrew people; a situation which recalls the personal relationship between the Sumerians and their inner personal god.

Verse 6
And the Lord said, Behold, the people is one, and they have all one language;...

The sons of Shem are a single people and they all speak the same language. That was true of the Sumerians for some seven hundred years after their city states had become established around or shortly before 3000BC. Sumerian remained the spoken language of Sumer probably until the Akkadian conquest and dynasty about 2300BC. Verse 6 continues:

...and this they begin to do; and now nothing will be restrained from them, which they have imagined to do.

The sons of Shem have built their cities with their towers, and with that achieved they will, in time, be able to do almost anything. In other words, the powers they will acquire as a result of creating a city civilisation will enable them to challenge the authority of God. The insight which inspired the scribes to write that, around 1100BC borders on prophecy. But an accusation of pride before God usually indicates pride among men. Kramer (The Sumerians, pp.267 ff.) is not the only one to doubt whether the Sumerians were greatly loved

Verse 7
Go to, let us go down, and there confound their language, that they may not understand one another's speech.

The sons of Shem begin to speak different languages so they could no longer all understand or communicate with each other. This deep memory of the loss of a common language reflects the decline and extinction of Sumerian as the spoken language of Sumer, which happened while the Sumerians still existed as an identifiable people. Akkadian began to be spoken widely in Sumer as well as in Akkad before *c.*2300BC when King Sargon of Akkad conquered the whole region. After the conquest, Akkadian was made the official language of both Sumer and Akkad. Two hundred years later, Akkadian was the main language of Sumer while Sumerian was becoming the classical language of learning and literature. During the next century, *c.*2100–2000BC, when the Sumerians briefly re-established supremacy, Sumerian was revived as the language of official documents, but after the destruction of Ur Sumerian was hardly spoken and Akkadian had finally triumphed.

The loss of their language marked the beginning of the end of the Sumerians as an identifiable people. No wonder it left a scar on the national consciousness, deep enough to be recorded in the Bible as a principal memory of their people.

Babel is Babylon. The name Babil is not found in the tablets before about 2300BC, but the settlement at the site where that city would later be built is very old indeed. Babylon did not acquire imperial stature until around 1800BC and the rise of Hammurabi, but to the scribes collating historical material under Moses in the south of Palestine around 1100BC, the city of Babylon was very much the centre and symbol both of their own contemporary culture and of the culture of ancient Sumer and Akkad. So Babylon symbolised the region from which the Hebrews recalled that their ancestors had come.

Once Shem has been identified with Sumer, the story of Shem as preserved in Genesis, Chapter 11, can hardly be other than the story of the Sumerians. Not only does the biblical record as now understood tally almost perfectly with the discoveries of archaeology, but a second biblical message becomes apparent: the Bible wishes to remind the Hebrews forever not just that their ancestors came from Sumer, but that they were the Sumerians.

CHAPTER 6

THE STRATEGY FOR SURVIVAL

Post-Sumer from *c.*2000/*c.*1800BC until after the Exodus

> I have come to understand that adherence to religious practice is not just a passing phase in Jewish history. It is an elemental means of preserving the Jewish people – and that, for me, is a basic value in itself.
>
> (Teddy Kollek, with his son Amos Kollek, *Jerusalem – A Life*)

The strategy for their survival as a cultural and ethnic entity, which the Hebrew people would now evolve, must so profoundly affect daily life that future generations would remain aware that they were a separate people long after they had forgotten about Sumer. They must be willing to impose on each other forever the necessary discipline, so the beliefs and practices which made up their strategy must be sanctified into a religion. And that, over a period of about six centuries, is what they did. Some of their practices and beliefs can now be

belief in the spiritual nature of both God and man. The consequences of that belief would become clear as soon as time, or some crucial event, should force them to choose between the traditional pantheon and their personal god. The crucial event was to be no less than the destruction of Sumer.

At some time between c.2000 and c.1800BC when the future offered only the final disappearance of their people, a few survivors, who the Bible calls Terah and Abraham, gathered together and set out for a new land. They were determined, whatever the cost, to preserve their Sumerian descent, to keep alive in their own persons and in their descendants forever, the originating genius of Sumer.

Religion would be vital. The Sumerian personal god contained, latent within, it all the ingredients needed for the ultimate spiritual, single and therefore supreme, God which the Jews were soon to be the first to worship. That would begin to happen as soon as their belief in the pantheon had crumbled in the smoke and rubble of Ur. Then the concept of a personal, spiritual god could be released from the pantheon and remain for them the sole, the single universal God of all mankind.

The refugees had abandoned the great gods of the pantheon because, when the crisis came, the gods had abandoned them. Without its gods the pantheon was meaningless. But the personal god was by birth part of the nature of each one of them forever, the one god they could never abandon, and that in the end was the God they kept.

A covenant with God

'The idea of a covenant between a deity and a people is unknown from other religions and cultures' (*Encyclopaedia Judaica*, 1971 Vol. 5, p.1021).

A covenant with Almighty God takes some accounting for, few if any nations have wished, let alone dared, to make such a claim. History can recall divine kings aplenty. Divine national missions have been more rare, and have usually ended in military defeat. A covenant is neither of those. Under a covenant, humanity and divinity retain their separate natures, but there is an explicit bond between them; and in so far as that bond is exclusive, a spirit of community is created among those included within the covenant, while a spirit of resentment is aroused among those excluded from it. A covenant can be a dangerous instrument.

The first covenant was made by God with every living creature including mankind, and was in no way exclusive to the Jews. It was communicated by God to Noah and its single clause was: no more floods (Gen. 9:11). It was sealed with a rainbow (Gen. 9:13).

The second covenant was with Abraham when he was ninety-nine years old, and it was the first exclusively with the Hebrew people. Its main terms were (Gen. 17:10-21):

-The covenant will be everlasting.
-To Abraham and his descendants will be given the land of Canaan as an everlasting possession.
-Boys are to be circumcised when eight days old if they are members of the family or are living in the house.
-Ishmael, Abraham's eldest son by Hagar the Egyptian serving maid, will multiply and beget twelve princes; but God will establish His covenant with Isaac, Abraham's son by Sarah his Hebrew wife.

The third covenant with Abraham's son Isaac, and the fourth covenant with Isaac's younger son Jacob, are essentially renewals of Abraham's covenant. They confirm the Hebrews' special relationship with God and the promise that they will be given the land of Canaan

The first four commandments define the concept of God and his place in the life, not just the religious life, of the Jews. They lay down the exclusive nature of the Jewish religion, and prescribe a regular and frequent ceremony to remind them of it, though not its precise form.

The fifth commandment guards the family. The last five commandments are, for their time, an astonishing enunciation of the moral basis of conduct. Astonishing, not because the principles are themselves new, but because for the very first time in history a god (or God) prescribes as law a specifically moral code. Gone are the days when law can express what wise judges have actually decided in representative cases. From now on, law will be based on principle backed by divine authority; the temple will guard the conscience of both palace and people, and the priest will lay down the parameters within which alone the civil power can govern and remain moral. Founded upon these five commandments, the concept of universal moral authority will generate centuries of conflict between church and state; and when the inquiring mind of science erodes the mystical influence of church, a secular moral sense will arise which will turn out to be wide open to political abuse. But through it all, the feeling that only an acceptable morality can justify law, will survive, as societies struggle towards, but never quite reach, justice.

This Jewish contribution to religious thought, enunciated in the ten commandments, was to be the foundation not only of subsequent

Solomon's Temple in Jerusalem, A nineteenth century reconstruction

Judaism, but also of Christianity and Islam. That was the measure of their achievement; and it evolved, maybe consciously, out of desperation following the destruction of Ur and Sumer; out of the resolute determination shown by Terah and his son, Abraham, as they and their little party struggled north-west to Haran, some time between c.2000 and c.1800BC.

The covenants with God fall into a pattern. The first covenant with Noah followed the flood, a time of disaster and dispersion. It promised the security of no more floods. That was before the Sumerian period. During the Sumerian period there were no covenants. The second covenant, with Abraham, was made during the long aftermath of their departure from Sumer when they had lost their homeland. The renewal covenants with Isaac and with Jacob were during their homeless wanderings in Canaan. The fifth covenant, with Moses, came after their departure from slavery in Egypt when they were wandering in Sinai with no fixed home.

All five covenants were made during periods of wandering and dispersion, when lack of a homeland would have been most keenly felt. But during the Sumerian period, from after the Flood to Abraham, when the Sumerians/Hebrews had their homeland in Sumer, there were no covenants. Of the post-Sumerian covenants, three specifically promise the Hebrews the land of Canaan as a homeland, while the

Jewish people and inspire them to preserve their Sumerian ancestry for centuries after they had forgotten about Sumer, there could be no compromise. They must hold themselves, and their children, in a discipline of steel so totally apart from the people around them that confrontation and war would be inevitable.

Moses recognised that the doctrine of a covenant with God implied a dangerous isolation, and in one of his conversations with God, he pleads:

> ...so shall we be separated, I and thy people, from all the people that are upon the face of the earth. (Exod.33:16)

This does not in any way mean that God is the exclusive property of the Jews; but by holding to a special relationship with God, the Jews will find themselves isolated from the rest of mankind. With unbelievable foresight, Moses warns that this will be dangerous.

The pantheon would have to be confronted, hence the first commandment, clear and uncompromising, 'Thou shalt have no other gods before me', and the second, 'Thou shalt not make unto thee any graven image'. These were reinforced by desperate instructions:

> Ye shall utterly destroy all the places, wherein the nations which ye shall possess served their gods...
> ...And ye shall overthrow their altars, and break their pillars, and burn their groves with fire, and ye shall hew down the graven images of their gods, and destroy the names out of them out of that place (Deut. 12:2-3)

Peace and tolerance will be replaced by war, the first religious war in recorded history. So in a land where they might have settled as peaceful immigrants, they arrived as conquerors.

How could this make sense if they were all blood brothers? The power of divine revelation will move a prophet to attempt conversion and disciples to die for the faith, but a cold policy of belligerent isolation needs different fuel. That fuel is supplied if they were descendants of Sumer, still aware of what their ancestors had created, conscious of a like ability in themselves, and knowing the history as well as the contemporary relevance of the single, spiritual God. As the surviving heirs of Sumer, aggressive, creative, resolute, they raise their national standard to their God; the only God that can (and will) preserve them. For their survival as a people the Jews needed a jealous God. From now on they would have one.

A ban on marriage outside the group

As the Hebrews considered themselves to be an elite people, the purity of their race was important to them. The tribe was small so that meant marrying cousins and sometimes travelling long distances to find them. Isaac, son of Abraham and Sarah, was sent to Padanaram to choose a wife from among the family of his uncle Nahor, who had stayed in Sumer when Terah and Abraham left. In the next generation, Esau, Isaac's eldest son, was not so amenable as his younger brother, Jacob, to whom he later sold his birthright. Miracles cannot go on happening for ever... Esau married two Hittite wives '...which were a grief of mind unto Isaac and unto Rebekah.' (Gen. 26:35). Jacob, the younger and more obedient of Isaac's two sons, but now with the status of firstborn, went to Padanaram to find his wife. In the event, he married two wives, Leah and Rachel, who were sisters, also from the family of Nahor.

If a Hebrew boy or girl marries out, even today, there will be a frown and then a sigh. It is not just a fear that differing religious practices can generate conflict inside a family, give rise to compromise solutions, and dilute religious observance especially among the young. Plenty of religions, Catholic, Protestant, Islam prefer marriage within 'the church'; for them, religion is what matters, and racial origin is irrelevant. For Hebrews, the personal religious beliefs of the boy and girl are less important than their parentage. If both are of good Hebrew descent, they may worship seaweed and socially all will be well. They may both be Jewish by religious belief, but if one is not a Hebrew by descent there will be lowered voices.

The Hebrews were not alone in requiring marriage within the group, but in imposing this rule they were acting against the custom of their age and place. Three kings of the Sumerian Third Dynasty of Ur (c.2100– 1900BC) had married Akkadian, Amar Sin, Shu Sin, Ibbi Sin. Whether they were semitic or not (the matter is not decisive), intermarriage between the Sumerians and the Akkadians had been common for centuries and was repugnant to neither. None of the surviving fragments of early law codes, including Hammurabi's, mentions intermarriage between races at all.

The semitic people of Canaan were willing to intermarry with the Hebrews, but the Hebrews were not willing to intermarry with them. On the face of it, it is very odd that this one small group alone among the peoples around them should have provocatively rejected intermarriage with their neighbours, on whose goodwill their survival depended.

It is odd but not unique. Plenty of small tribal groups, feeling themselves threatened, have insisted on marriage within the tribe; especially those living in a difficult or separate physical environment. A ban on intermarriage might be remarkable, but it would not be exceptional. But their ban on intermarriage was only one policy among many. No other separate tribal group has proclaimed, as a coherent programme, belief in a single almighty God, an exclusive covenant with God, war against their neighbour's religions, as well as a ban on marriage outside the group. The Jewish policy on marriage taken in isolation would be easily explained; their total strategy including their ban on intermarriage is not.

The strategy for survival

The existence of a strategy, the inevitable consequence of which must be separation from their semitic neighbours, raises the question whether the Hebrews were a semitic people at all – a question which the world so emphatically answers but never properly asks. The suggestion that they were Aramaeans can be easily discounted on dates;

CHAPTER 7

SUMMARY

BUT THAT does not prove it. The evidence must be briefly reviewed and a balance struck.

The background from which the strategy for survival arose was the absorption of the (non-semitic) Sumerians by the (semitic) Akkadians, a process which continued for centuries and resulted in the Sumerian language being no longer the spoken language of Sumer. The event which jolted the remaining Sumerians into actually constructing the strategy was their departure from Sumer following the destruction of Ur around 2000BC, which left them without a homeland. The outline of the strategy was evolved bit by bit over the succeeding centuries. It consisted of beliefs and rules governing all aspects of their lives of which four only have been considered here:

> Belief in a single, spiritual and universal God.
> War against the religions of their neighbours.
> A covenant between God and their people.
> A ban on marriage outside the group.

To these four policies Moses added the ten commandments, which defined the practical relationship between God and the Jews and made it clear that the basis for correct living must be a moral law.

This formed an astonishing programme within which a small group of people could preserve their identity, and find continuing fulfilment for their religious aspirations and their social ideals. A unique blend of rigidity of principle and universality of scope has enabled the programme to last, virtually unchanged, for four thousand years.

The Sumerians knew the quality of the civilisation they had built; and the survivors were aware that they still nursed in themselves the innate ability of their ancestors. The Sumerians had compared their cities and the ordered lives within them, their assured supply of food, the great buildings, the laws which ruled them, the schools which many of their children went to, the fruits of literacy and numeracy which were tangible in their lives, the science, the songs, the tales, the poetry — all this they compared with the quality of life in the sur-

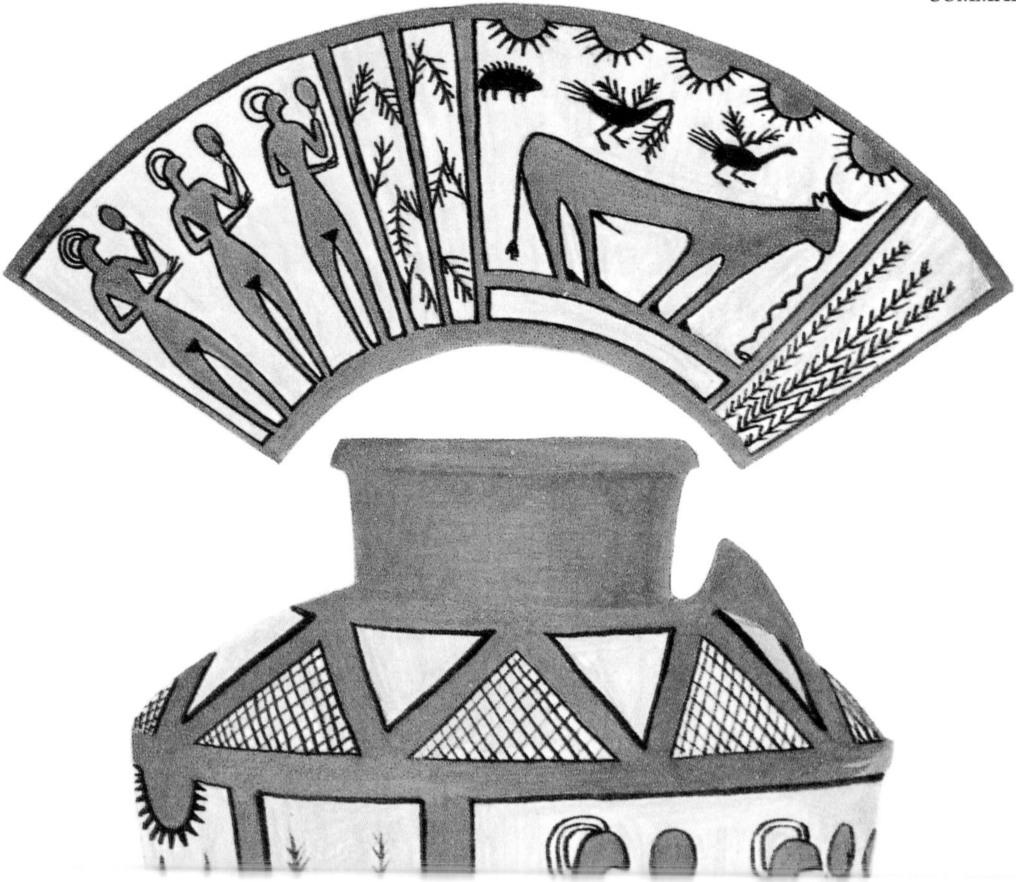

tlements and camps of the desert immigrants arriving in Sumer from the west and they must have lived with fear.

So they learnt how to preserve the civilisation they had created. The meticulous copying in their schools, the detailed recording in treasury and storehouse, the laws themselves, so much of what has survived from Sumer tells us they knew they held it all in precarious possession, and that to preserve it had to be their first duty to themselves, their children and to the world.

When their cities lay in ruins, the Sumerians all but gone, of course the few survivors came together with a single purpose: to preserve their people and plant their seed afresh. So they left not only Sumer but the whole of that valley and went far away north west to Haran.

The Bible says that the Hebrews were descended from Abraham, and that Abraham, whether a person or a name standing for a group, came from Ur of the Chaldees. Why, then, has the possibility that they might have been Sumerians never, even today, been seriously considered?

Until the middle of the last century, modern man knew nothing of Sumer, not even its name. The name Sumer does not occur in the Bible; Akkad does, but the Bible gives no clue to what or where it might have been. The child asking teacher or priest 'Please, what is Shinar?' was told, truthfully, 'We do not know'.

The evidence then available that the Hebrews were semitic was overwhelming. Their language, Hebrew, was semitic, so was their cultural affiliation as far back as recorded history could expose it; the Bible suggested it, or provided no basis for any other supposition. Confronted by the weight of circumstance how could a rational person contend otherwise? Why should he wish to? So, over the centuries, tradition hardened into fact.

When, in the middle of the last century, the decipherment of the ancient scripts led to the discovery of the Sumerian language, then of Sumer, when archaeology revealed the physical remains and scholars began to translate and interpret the tablets, when the story of Sumer began to be recorded, the tradition persisted; old belief was not adjusted to new knowledge, and the Hebrews continued to proclaim that they were a semitic people.

Archaeology has unburied, and continues to unbury, the clay tablets on which the Sumerians kept their records. Scholars continued with unbelievable self control gather the fragments, compare them, see where the messages fit, so the outline of the story of Sumer is reconstructed from the remains of their archives. Of the many things that those remains have told us, two are now crucial: that 'Shinar' indicates both Sumer and Akkad; that in cuneiform 'Sumer' is properly 'Shumer' and that it is from 'Shumer' that 'Shem' is almost certainly derived. That enables the history of Shem as recorded in the Bible to be recognised as the history of Sumer. Once that identification has been made, the correspondence between the biblical and the archaeological records is so nearly complete that there can be no further doubt:

☐ Bible tells us that Shem and his descendants came into the land known as Sumer and Akkad from the east. The evidence suggests that the Sumerians did enter from the east, and archaeologists are increasingly looking at the Indus as a possible area from which they might have come.

☐ The Bible tells us that the sons of Shem used burnt brick and bitumen for their buildings. Archaeology tells us that these were the building materials used by the Sumerians.

☐ The Bible tells us that the sons of Shem built a city with a tower, implying that they were the first to do so. The Sumerians built the first cities and ziggurats in Sumer and Akkad.

☐ The Bible tells us that the sons of Shem lost their language. So did the Sumerians.

the personal qualities of the parents are often reproduced in the children along with the physical characteristics of facial similarity and build. Moses foresaw that a racial policy would provoke dangerous hostility against them, but it was considered to be essential to their survival and it was maintained. Nowadays, it has become increasingly apparent that personal qualities derive as much from cultural environment as from ethnic descent; and that, over time, immigrants generally not only adapt to the way of life and ideals of the society in which they have been accepted, but develop their abilities so that they perform in their host society comparably with those whose ancestors had been born within it. As with the Sumerians and Akkadians, societies intermingled with each other tend to draw together culturally, and if minorities seek to preserve a language or customs they are seldom permanently successful. It is the more remarkable that the Jews, although living intermingled with other people, should have evolved, set down in writing, and sustained a programme which was designed to keep them rigidly separate; and it is scarcely less remarkable that no serious attempt to account for it is even now being made.

During the centuries after their arrival in Haran, the Jews constructed a strategy for their survival as a nation. That strategy involved embedding as a religion deep in the very centre of their lives beliefs and daily practices which would keep them culturally and ethnically distinct from all other peoples. The physical achievements of Sumer lay buried in the ashes of their cities, but over the centuries which followed that destruction two attributes emerged as crucial: the innate creativity of the Sumerian people; the concept of a single, spiritual and universal God which they had evolved out of the personal god of their Sumerian ancestors. These two had to be preserved no matter what the cost might turn out to be. The principle needs of their strategy can be listed:

☐ They would need to believe they were the one of chosen people.

☐ They would need to believe in the concept of a single, spiritual and universal God which, being evolved from the ancient personal god of their ancestors, would bind together the traditional with the modern, the individual with the nation

☐ They would need a God who would be real in their lives and offer them a measure of security. They evolved the doctrine of covenants between God and themselves whose main recurrent features were that God recognised a special relationship with them and promised that an attainable homeland, the land of Canaan, would be given to them.

☐ They would need a jealous God to protect them against the lure of assimilation by forbidding them, for instance, to follow other gods or marry outside the group.

☐ They would need a God whose damnation they would fear, because fear of breaking out of the group would help to keep the group together.

☐ They would need a God to love, so that through a common love they would feel themselves to be deeply involved in, and part of, each other.

Out of these needs grew the policies which together formed their strategy for survival, of which these are four:

☐ They must worship only the single, spiritual and universal God.

☐ They must make war against other religions, and especially against those who worshipped the gods of the ancient pantheon.

☐ They must obey the terms of the covenants between God and their

CHAPTER 8

REFLECTIONS

A PRACTICAL ACCOUNT of how some beliefs central to the Jewish religion may have come to be held does not mean that those beliefs in themselves were no more than expedients. Religious perception has a long history, and the possibility that it may be real cannot lightly be dismissed. In the extremity of peril, people will clutch at straws and then, very occasionally they discover, to their amazement, that they have grasped a truth.

The truth which the Hebrews grasped while tending their flocks in Canaan was that life has a spiritual dimension which is universal and therefore moral, which can be perceived by, and is related to, individuals directly. This understanding, in the form of a spiritual and universal God, emerged from the Sumerian concept of a personal God and became the core of the Jewish religion. The destruction of Sumer released this concept from the pantheon, but the determination of the remaining Sumerians to survive as an entity caused it to be embedded in their new strategy of racial purity. As Moses had forewarned, a policy of racial purity was dangerous, though the strategy was successful and its purpose not ignoble.

After Sumer, the binding force of their society was their religion, to stick together their overriding need. The only god they still had, the god they kept, was their personal god, always spiritual, intimate, passing from father to son, a bond between the generations. When a new need for wider unity opened their minds to the vision of a single universal God, they recognised that as a more profound expression of ancient religious experience, the vital link between the old world of Sumer and their future as Jews.

They could not yet guess that this universal concept was to seize the heart of half the world and inspire two more great spiritual religions, Christianity and Islam. But what is forged in desperation is apt to endure.

Belief in a benign universality of spirit, while very possibly correct, would not suffice for their immediate, let alone their long-term, practical needs. From Haran on they needed claws as well. What they evolved was a special direct relationship with a spiritual God of such an aggressive nature as to separate them permanently, almost disastrously, from their neighbours. They knew the sort of price they would have to pay to preserve their separate cultural identity, but perhaps not how long and bitter the payment would prove to be.

Religion came first but it was not all. We have seen how their faith underpinned a strategy of physical separateness which made enemies of would-be friends and destroyed their hopes for even a fragile security. How could it ever be supposed that these were a semitic people, just one group formed at random from among their fellows with no ethnic, cultural or historical justification?

After Sumer, they were careful about a priesthood. The gods of the pantheon had been served by priests, but the Sumerian personal god had not. That was an inner presence, an indivisible part of each person, leaving neither room nor need for priest. The larger vision, to which they came under pressure of crisis, retained the innate affinity between God and man and similarly excluded any role for a priesthood. So they had learned men, called Rabbi's, to guard the sacred precincts, officiate at public ceremonies, to advise, to guide; but no priesthood to stand between the person and his God.

We speak about temperament, and observe that the aggressive

Ram in the thicket, actually a goat, in gold leaf and lapis lazuli. It is one of a pair from Ur, c.2600BC, whose use is unknown.

A representation of a menorah, the Jewish sacred lamp, which is described in the Bible. From a fourteenth-century French manuscript, reproduced by Joan Comay in *The Temple of Jerusalem*.

gave their concept of a universal and spiritual God to the world, but maintained their racial strategy and kept themselves apart. This policy may have preserved some of the originating genius of Sumer but for it the rest of the world has always exacted and continues to exact a very high price.

For too many centuries the Hebrew people have been precarious guests in other peoples' lands, forced either to lose their identity or preserve it by means which must, and do, cause bitter offence. So persecution has followed. As a result, their own inner pride has been eroded and they too often hear the word 'Jew' as either a curse or an embarrassment.

Though the experts are quite properly diffident about suggesting conclusions which the facts have not already established for them, an outsider with nothing to lose can take a risk, look across many fields, and say without fear what the outline suggests to him. And the outline, now delineated equally by the Bible and by archaeology, suggests very clearly that the Jews are the descendants of the ancient Sumerians.

Knowledge that it was the ancestors of the Jews who entered Sumer six and half thousand years ago and who, a thousand years later, began to create in Sumer the oldest civilisation known to history; that for four thousand years of persecution since leaving Sumer, the descendants of those ancestors have preserved themselves as a people and preserved, however faint, traces of their magnificent past; knowledge that, for all the new and different blood that has flowed into the Jewish people, they are still identifiable as a group, still able to move deserts to fertility and people to exasperation, still vital, still creative: all this must at least help to sweep away the remnants of acquired diffidence and win at last a real acceptance from the world.

APPENDICES

APPENDIX 1 SOME OF THE DYNASTIES IN SUMER AND AKKAD

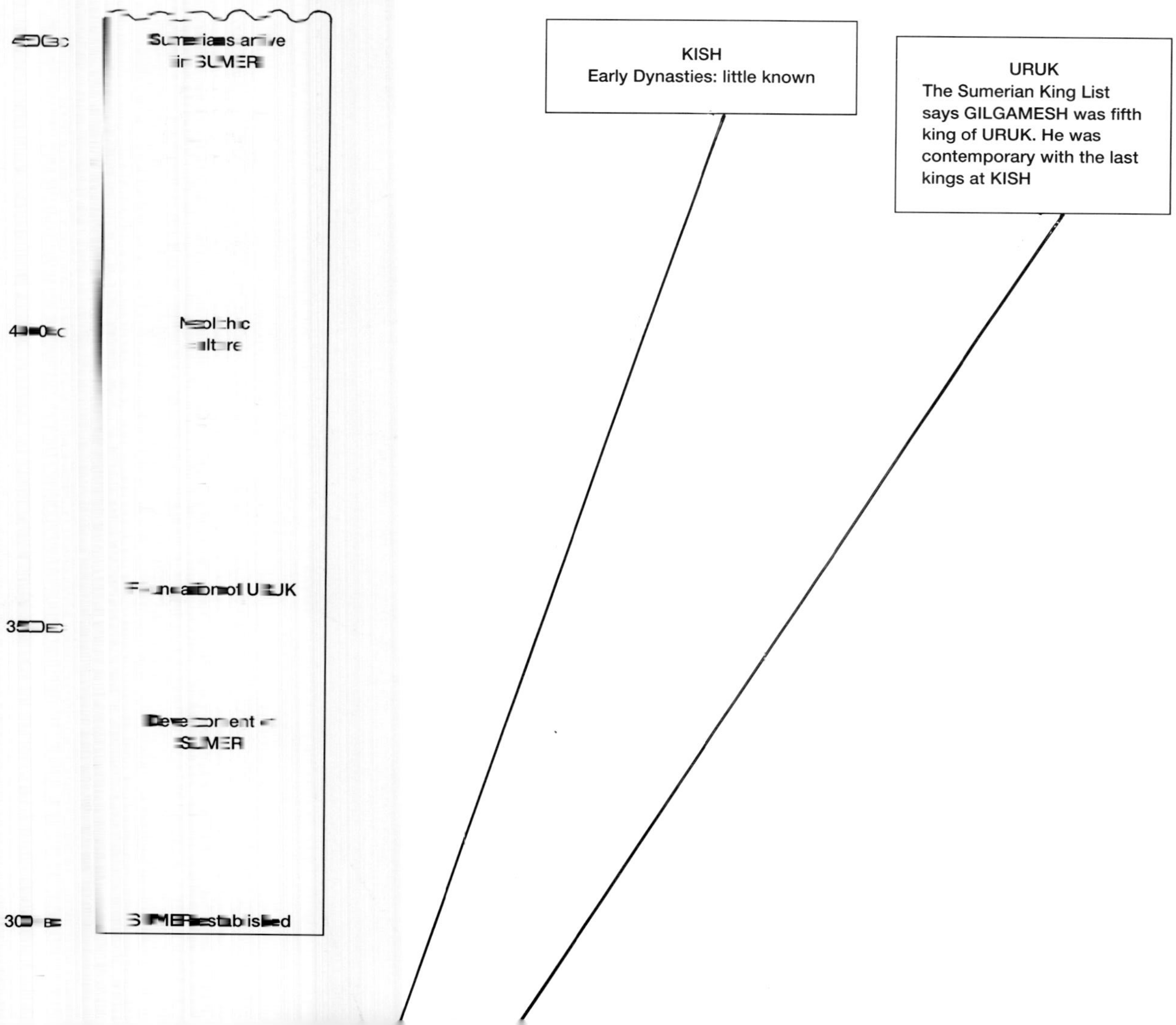

KISH
Early Dynasties: little known

URUK
The Sumerian King List says GILGAMESH was fifth king of URUK. He was contemporary with the last kings at KISH

Sumerians arrive in SUMER

Neolithic culture

Fall and rise of URUK

Dependent SUMER

SUMER established

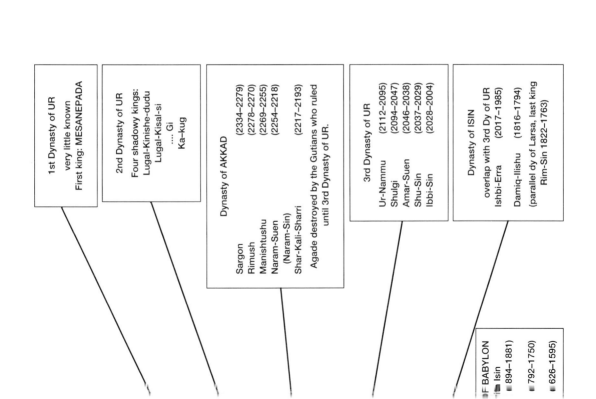

1st Dynasty of UR
very little known
First king: MESANEPADA

2nd Dynasty of UR
Four shadowy kings:
Lugal-Kinishe-dudu
Lugal-Kisal-si
..... Gi
Ka-kug

Dynasty of AKKAD

Sargon   (2334–2279)
Rimush   (2278–2270)
Manishtushu   (2269–2255)
Naram-Suen   (2254–2218)
(Naram-Sin)
Shar-Kali-Sharri (2217–2193)

Agade destroyed by the Gutians who ruled
until 3rd Dynasty of UR.

3rd Dynasty of UR

Ur-Nammu   (2112–2095)
Shulgi   (2094–2047)
Amar-Suen   (2046–2038)
Shu-Sin   (2037–2029)
Ibbi-Sin   (2028–2004)

Dynasty of ISIN

overlap with 3rd Dy of UR
Ishbi-Erra   (2017–1985)

Damiq-Ilishu (1816–1794)
(parallel dy of Larsa, last king
Rim-Sin 1822–1763)

BABYLON
Isin   894–1881)
        792–1750)
        626–1595)

APPENDIX 2 WHAT 18 BIBLES OR COMMENTARIES SAY ABOUT THE ORIGIN OF THE HEBREWS

Title	Original source	Edition quoted	Wording under Genesis 11:2
FROM THE EAST Jewish versions			
The Septuagint	Derived from original text about 250BC	Samuel Bagster edition, undated, perhaps about 1900	"And all the earth was of one lip, and there was one language to all. And it came to pass as they moved from the east, they found a plain in the land of Senaar, and they dwelt there".
Midrash Rabbah	Genesis Rabbah. A commentary on the Torah, c.AD400–500.	Translated with notes under the editorship of Rabbi Dr H. Freedman and Maurice Simon, 1951.	"And it came to pass as they journeyed from the east." Comment: 'They travelled from further east to nearer east.' Footnote: 'Since they came to Shinar (Babylon) which is in the east, the Rabbi's maintain that they travelled from a still more easterly point.'
Ramban (Nachmanides)	Commentary on the Torah. 'Rabbi Moshe ben Nachman... laid the foundation for the Jewish community in Jerusalem...AD1267	Translated and annotated by Rabbi Dr Charles B. Chavel, 1971	"As they journeyed from the east...".
The pentateuch	The five books of Moses	Translated and explained by Samson Raphael Hirsch, 1959.	"And it came to pass as they journeyed from the east, that they found a plain in the land of Shinar, and they dwelt there."
Anchor Bible	Translation and notes. Introduction: "The present translation bears... close resemblance to the version by the Jewish Publication Society of America (1962)'	Translated by E.A. Speiser, 1964.	"As men migrated from the east, they came upon a valley in the land of Shinar and settled there,"
The Living Torah	A new translation based on traditional Jewish sources. 1981	Translated by Rabbi Aryeh Kaplan 1981	"When (the people) migrated from the east, they found a valley in the land of Shinar, and they settled there."

Title	Original source	Edition quoted	Wording under Genesis 11:2
FROM THE EAST Non-Jewish Versions			
The Vulgate	Derived from a text of about the 4th century AD.	Samuel Bagster edition, undated, perhaps about 1900.	"Cunque profiscerentur de oriente, invenerunt campus in terra Senaar, et habitaverunt in eo." Author's translation: "When they set out from the east, they found a plain in the land Senaar, and they dwelt there."
The Holy Bible (Authorised Version)	Translated under the instructions of King James I (1566–1625)	Text published in 1611.	"And it came to pass, as they journeyed from the east, that they found a plain in the land of Shinar; and they dwelt there."
Douay Version	Translated from the Latin Vulgate	Rheims 1582 and Douay 1609	"And when they removed from the east, they found a plain in the land of Senaar, and dwelt in it."
The Moffat Translation of the Bible		1934 edition; 1964 impression.	"In the days when the whole earth had one language and one vocabulary, there was a migration from the east, and men came

Title	Original source	Edition quoted	Wording under Genesis 11:2
NON-COMMITTAL Non-Jewish Versions			
Revised Version	A revision of the Authorised Version, researched 1881–86, 1901 and 1952.	Edition 1952.	"And as men migrated in the east, they found a plain in the land of Shinar and settled there."
The New English Bible	A general revision, 1970.	Edition 1970	"As men journeyed in the east, they came upon a plain in the land of Shinar and settled there."
The Cambridge Bible Commentary	A commentary on the biblical text	By Robert Davidson, 1973.	"As men journeyed in the east, they came upon...".
FROM THE WEST Jewish Versions			
The Holy Scriptures according to the Massoretic Text		Edition 1917.	"And it came to pass, as they journeyed east, that they found a plain in the land of Shinar; and they dwelt there."
The Pentateuch and Haftorahs	Hebrew text, English translation and commentary	Edited by the late Chief Rabbi, Dr J.H. Hertz CH, 1950.	"And it came to pass as they journeyed east that they found a plain in the land of Shinar, and they dwelt there."
FROM THE WEST Non-Jewish Versions			
La Bible de Jérusalem	Prepared by the Dominican Bible School in Jerusalem, 1956.	Edition 1973	"Comme les hommes se deplacaient à l'orient...." Author's translation: "As men travelled to the east".
The Jerusalem Bible	The English version of La Bible de Jérusalem was published in 1966. It was 'not entirely faithful rendering of the original textum' and preserved (for the most part) the interpretation adopted by the School in the light of the most recent researches in history, archaeology and literary criticism.	Edition 1968	"Now as they moved eastwards..."

BIBLIOGRAPHY

ABDULWALID, ALI FADHIL. *Sumerian Letters: Two Collections from the Old Babylonian Schools.* University of Pennsylvania PhD 1964, University Microfilms, Ann Arbor, Michigan

ADAMS, ROBERT MC.C. Ancient Mespotamian Settlement Patterns and the Problems of Urban Origins, *Sumer* XXV, 1969

ALLBRIGHT, W.F. From the Patriarchs to Moses, *The Biblical Archaeologist*, Vol.36, No.1, February 1973 (*posthumous*)

ALSTER, BENDT. The Instructions of Suruppak: A Sumerian Proverb Collection (Abu Salabikh version). Mespotamia: *Copenhagen Studies in Assyriology*, Vol. 2, 1974 (Akademisk Forlag, Copenhagen)

BARTON, GEORGE A. *Sumerian Business and Administrative Documents from the Earliest Times to the Dynasty of Agade*, University Museum, Philadelphia, 1915

BERMANT, CHAIM AND WEITZMAN, MICHAEL. *Ebla*, Weidenfeld and Nicolson, London, 1979

BIBBY, GEOFFREY. *Looking for Dilmun*, Collins, 1970

BOWMAN, RAYMOND A. Aramaeans, Aramaic and the Bible *Journal of Near Eastern Studies*, Vol. VII, April 1948, No.2

BOYER, CARL B. *A History of Mathematics*, John Wiley and Sons Inc, USA 1968

BUTTERFIELD, HERBERT. *The Origins of History*, Eyre Methuen, 1981

FRYMER-KENSKY, TIKVA. God Before the Hebrews, *The Biblical Archaeologist*, Vol. 8, No.5, September 1982

GADD, CYRIL J. *Teachers and Students in the Oldest Schools*, School of Oriental and African Studies, University of London, 1956

GOETZE, ALBRECHT. Fifty Old Babylonian Letters from Harmal, *Sumer*, Vol. XIV, 1958

GORDON, CYRUS H. *Before the Bible*, Collins, 1962

GORDON, CYRUS H. Where is Abraham's Ur? *The Biblical Archaeologist*, Vol. 3 No.2, June 1977

GORDON, EDMUND I. *Sumerian Proverbs: Glimpses of Everyday Life in Ancient Mespotamia*, The University Museum of Pennsylvania, Philadelphia, 1959

GREEN, M.W. The Construction and Implementation of the Cuneiform Writing System, *Visible Language*, Vol. XV, Number 4, Autumn 1981

GURNEY, O.R. *The Hittites*, Penguin Books, 1975 edition

HALLO, W.W. The Individual Prayer in Sumerian: The Continuity of a Tradition, *Journal of the American Oriental Society*, No. 88, 1968

HALLO, W.W. Toward a History of Sumerian Literature, Sumerological Studies in Honor of Thorkild Jacobson on his Seventieth Birthday, June 7th 1974. *Assyriological Studies*, No 20, University of Chicago Press, 1975

HARDEN, DONALD. *The Phoenicians*, Thames and Hudson, 1962

HARRISON, R.K. *Introduction to the Old Testament*, The Tyndale Press, 1970

HAWKES, JACQUETTA. Dawn of the Gods, Chatto & Windus, 1968

HAWKES, JACQUETTA. *The First Great Civilisations*, Hutchinson, 1973

HEATON, E.W. *Solomon's New Men*, Thames and Hudson, 1974

HELD, GEORGE F. Parallels between The Gilgamesh Epic and Plato's Symposium, *Journal of Near Eastern Studies*, Vol. 42, 1983

JACOBSEN, THORKILD. *Treasures of Darkness*, Yale University Press, 1976

JONES, THOMAS B. (Editor) *The Sumerian Problem*, John Wiley and Sons Inc, 1969

JONES, THOMAS B. Sumerian Administrative Documents: Sumerological Studies in Honor of Thorkild Jacobsen on his Seventieth Birthday, June 7th 1974. *Assyriological Studies* No 20, University of Chicago Press, 1975

KELLER, WERNER. *The Bible as History* (Trans. William Mell DD) Hodder and Stoughton, 1956, 1974 Edition

KIRNAST, BURKHART. The Name of the City of Babylon, *Sumer*, Vol. 35, 1979

KRAELING, EMIL G.H. *Aram and Israel*, AMS Press, Inc., New York, 1966

KRAMER, SAMUEL NOAH. Schooldays, A Sumerian Composition Relating to the Education of a Scribe, *Journal of the American Oriental Society*, Vol. 69 No 4, October-December, 1949

KRAMER, SAMUEL NOAH. *The Sumerians*, The University of Chicago Press, 1963

KRAMER, SAMUEL NOAH. The 'Babel of Tongues', A Sumerian Version, *Journal of the American Oriental Society*, No.88, 1968

KRAMER, SAMUEL NOAH. History Begins at Sumer, The University of Pennsylvania Press, 1981

KRAMER, SAMUEL NOAH. The Ur-Nammu Law Code: Who Was Its Author? *Orientalia*, Vol. 2, Fasc.4, 1983

LAYARD, AUSTEN HENRY. *Nineveh and its Remains*, John Murray, 1849

LLOYD, SETON. *The Archaeology of Mespotamia*, Thames and Hudson, 1978

LADY MAGNUS. *Outlines of Jewish History*, Myers & Co, 1931

MALAMET, ABRAHAM. Mari, *The Biblical Archaeologist*, Vol. 34 No.1, 1971

MALLOWAN, M.E.L. *Early Mespotamia and Iran*, Thames and Hudson, 1965

MAZAR, BENJAMIN. The Aramaean Empire and its Relations with Israel, *The Biblical Archaeologist*, Vol. XXV No.4, 1962

MELAART, JAMES. *The Neolithic of the Ancient Near East*. London, Thames and Hudson, 1975

MICHALOWSKI, PIOTR. Review of 'Briefe aus dem Iraq Museum', Altbabylonische Briefe 8, Leiden, 1980, *Journal of Cuneiform Studies*, Vol. 35, 1983

MILLARD, ALAN R. A Wandering Aramaean, *Journal of Near Eastern Studies*, Vol. 39, 1980

MOOREY, P.R.S. *Kish Excavations 1923-1933*, Clarendon Press, Oxford, 1978, Reprinted 1979

MOOREY, P.R.S. Revised Edition of Sir Leonard Wooley's *Ur of the Chaldees*, Cornell University Press, 1982

MOSCATI, SABATINO. *Ancient Semitic Civilisations*, Elek Books Limited, 1957

MOSCATI, SABATINO. *The Face of the Ancient Orient*, Routledge, 1960

ROUX, GEORGES. *Ancient Iraq*, Pelican Books, 2nd edition 1980,
reprinted 1985

SAGGS, H.W.F. *Everyday Life in Babylonia and Assyria*, B.J. Batsford, 1965

SALONEN, A. *Die Ziegeleien in Alten Mespotamien*, Suomalainen Tiedeakatemia,
Helsinki, 1972

SANDARS, N.K. *The Sea People*, Thames and Hudson, 1978

SANDARS, N.K. *The Epic of Gilgamesh*, Penguin Books, 1983

SCHAEFFER, CLAUDE F.A. The Last Days of Ugarit, *The Biblical Archaeologist*,
Vol. 8, No 5, September 1983

SCHMANDT-BESSERAT, DENISE. From Token to Tablets: A Re-evaluation of the
so-called 'Numerical Tablets' *Visible Language*, Vol. XV, Number 4,
Autumn 1981

SHENDGE, MALATI J. The Use of Seals and the Invention of Writing, *Journal of
the Economic and Social History of the Orient*, Vol. XXVI, Part II, 1983

SHIN T. KANG *Sumerian Economic Texts from the Umma Archive*, University of
Illinois Press, 1973

SJÖBERG, A. The Old Babylonian Edubba: Sumerological Studies in Honor of
Thorkild Jacobsen on his Seventieth Birthday, June 7th 1974,
Assyriological Studies No.20, University of Chicago Press, 1975

SJÖBERG, A. In Praise of the Scribal Art, *Journal of Cuneiform Studies*, Vol. 24,
1972

SOLLBERGER, EDMOND. Some Legal Documents of the Third Dynasty of Ur, in
Kramer Anniversary Volume, Ed Barry L. Eichler, Verlag Butzon and
Becker Kenelaer, 1976

THESIGER, WILFRED. *The Marsh Arabs*, Longman, 1964

THOMPSON, THOMAS L. *The Historicity of the Patriarchal Narratives*, Walter de
Gruyter, 1974

THOMSEN, MARIE LOUISE. *The Sumerian Language*, Akademish Forlag
Copenhagen, 1974

VANSTIPHOUT, H.L.J. How Did They Learn Sumerian? *Journal of Cuneiform
Studies*, Vol. 31, 1979

WALKER, C.B.F. Another Babati Inscription, *Journal of Cuneiform Studies*,
Vol 35 1983

WALKER, C.B.F. *Cuneiform*, British Museum Publications, 1987

WALTERS, STANLEY D. *Water for Larsa (An Old Babylonian Archive dealing with
Irrigation)*, Yale University Press, 1970

WHITEHOUSE, RUTH. *The First Cities*, Phaidon Press, 1977

WURTHWEIN, ERNST. *The Text of the Old Testament – An Introduction to the
Biblia Hebraica*, translated by Erroll F Rhodes, SCM Press, London 1980

YADIN, YIGUEL. *Hazor*, Weidenfeld and Nicolson, 1975.

ILLUSTRATION
ACKNOWLEDGEMENTS

THE ILLUSTRATIONS used in this book are reproduced by kind permission of the following:

THE BRITISH MUSEUM, pp. 11, 15, 19, 23, 26, 27, 28, 34, 35, 39, 41, 45, 49, 53, *(top & bottom)*, 56, 57, 59, 61, 63

THAMES & HUDSON, pp. 24, 51, 85, 105

MR C.B.F. WALKER, p. 29

INDEX